UNIVERSITY OF KANSAS

MUSEUM OF NATURAL HISTORY

PUBLIC EDUCATION SERIES No. 6

October 21, 1977

THE AMPHIBIANS OF MISSOURI

By Tom R. Johnson
Missouri Dept. of Conservation
Jefferson City, Mo. 65101

UNIVERSITY OF KANSAS
LAWRENCE
1977

UNIVERSITY OF KANSAS PUBLICATIONS,
MUSEUM OF NATURAL HISTORY

Editor: E. O. Wiley
Co-Editor: Rebecca A. Pyles

PUBLIC EDUCATION SERIES No. *6*
pp. 1-142; 67 figures, 42 maps
Published October 21, 1977

ISBN: 0-89338-005-9

TO MY WIFE DIANE

AND

TO MY PARENTS.

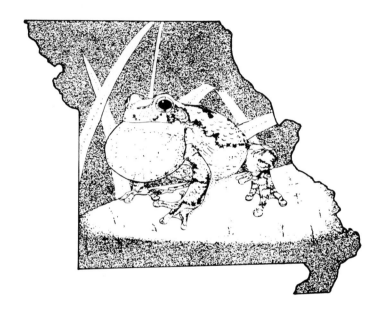

PREFACE

It has been 66 years since a book has been published on the amphibians of Missouri (Hurter, 1911), and to date no comprehensive work is available on this subject.

In the last few years there has been increased interest in our natural resources, and people are becoming more aware of the beautiful natural heritage of this country: the wild flora and fauna. More importantly, there is growing interest in finding ways to preserve our wildlife, and one way to accomplish this is to have an informed public. *The Amphibians of Missouri* has been written for this reason. There are presently 48 species and subspecies of amphibians known to occur in Missouri. Several species are now protected by law, but this cannot be effective unless Missourians are able to identify the amphibians of their state.

I hope this work will be useful to the biologist and non-biologist alike, and that anyone who is interested in the natural history and distribution of these animals will find this book helpful. A comprehensive bibliography is furnished to assist the reader who wishes to learn more about the herpetofauna of Missouri.

During the three years of work on this project I had the help and cooperation of a number of people, and without their assistance this book would have never materialized. I am grateful to Robert N. Bader for first giving me the idea to write this book. Ronald A. Brandon, Joseph T. Collins, and Richard S. Funk critically read the manuscript and offered numerous and valuable suggestions. I am indebted to these persons for their interest, guidance, and unselfish efforts. For proof reading the manuscript I thank Carol L. Kramer. I am also grateful to Lauren E. Brown and Richard S. Funk for kindly supplying the gray treefrog sonograph.

I offer my thanks to the following persons who helped me in securing specimens or county records, helping in photographic problems, supplying reprints, for assistance in field work, and other kindnesses: Tom Aley, Robert N. Bader, Mr. and Mrs. Glenn F. Bartlett, George C. Becker, Jeffrey H. Black, Ronald A. Brandon, Lauren E. Brown, Mr. and Mrs. Bill Burkhalter, John Bursewicz, Charles J. Cole, Joseph T. Collins, Roger Conant, Mary E. Dawson, David A. Easterla, Daniel B. Fitzhenry, Jr., Richard S. Funk, Carl Gerhardt, Harry Gregory, J. Whitfield Gibbons, Bill Heckt, Mike P. Hemkens, Richard Highton, James G. Houser, Donald A. Kangas, Randy Krohmer, Richard L. Lardie, Larry L. Latimer, Bob and Linda Leis, Hymen Marx, Dean E. Metter, Claudia E. Mink, Michael A. Morris, Robert W. Murphy, Max A. Nickerson, Edward P. Ortleb, Dennis B. Ralin, Donald Rimbach, Owen J. Sexton,

Dorothy M. Smith, Philip W. Smith, Charles D. Sullivan, Terry Vandeventer, James L. Vial, Richard C. Vogt, Mr. and Mrs. Norman W. Woessner, Thomas G. Yahnke, George R. Zug, Richard G. Zweifel.

My thanks to the Museum of Natural History, the University of Kansas, for their efforts in seeing this book to publication.

Finally I would like to express a special thanks to my wife Diane who helped in so many ways during the evolution of this book, for help in the field, and for typing the entire manuscript. All funding for this work came from our personal income, and no person, foundation, or institution contributed any financial assistance whatever.

Tom R. Johnson
January, 1977
St. Louis, Missouri

CONTENTS

Introduction ⸺ 1

    Amphibian classification ⸺ 3

    Physiographic provinces of Missouri ⸺ 3

    Explanation of family and species accounts ⸺ 5

Checklist of Missouri Amphibians ⸺ 8

Key to the Amphibians of Missouri ⸺ 10

    Salamanders ⸺ 11

    Toads and frogs ⸺ 14

Salamander Families and Species Accounts:

    Family Cryptobranchidae, Giant Salamanders ⸺ 18

        Hellbender (*Cryptobranchus alleganiensis*) ⸺ 19

    Family Sirenidae, Sirens and Lesser Sirens ⸺ 21

        Western Lesser Siren (*Siren intermedia nettingi*) 22

    Family Ambystomatidae, Mole Salamanders ⸺ 24

        Ringed Salamander (*Ambystoma annulatum*) ⸺ 25

        Spotted Salamander (*Ambystoma maculatum*) ⸺ 27

        Marbled Salamander (*Ambystoma opacum*) ⸺ 29

        Mole Salamander (*Ambystoma talpoideum*) ⸺ 31

        Small-mouthed Salamander (*Ambystoma texanum*) ⸺ 33

        Eastern Tiger Salamander (*Ambystoma t. tigrinum*) ⸺ 35

    Family Salamandridae, Newts ⸺ 37

        Central Newt (*Notophthalmus v. louisianensis*) ⸺ 38

    Family Amphiumidae, Amphiumas ⸺ 41

        Three-toed Amphiuma (*Amphiuma tridactylum*) 42

    Family Plethodontidae, Lungless Salamanders ⸺ 44

        Long-tailed Salamander (*Eurycea longicauda*) ⸺ 45

        Cave Salamander (*Eurycea lucifuga*) ⸺ 47

        Gray-bellied Salamander (*Eurycea multiplicata griseogaster*) ⸺ 49

        Oklahoma Salamander (*Eurycea tynerensis*) ⸺ 51

Four-toed Salamander (*Hemidactylium scutatum*) 52

Ozark Red-backed Salamander (*Plethodon dorsalis angusticlavius*) 54

Slimy Salamander (*Plethodon g. glutinosus*) 56

Southern Red-backed Salamander (*Plethodon serratus*) 58

Grotto Salamander (*Typhlotriton spelaeus*) 60

Family Proteidae, Mudpuppy and Waterdogs 62

Mudpuppy (*Necturus maculosus*) 63

Toad and Frog Families and Species Accounts:

Family Pelobatidae, Spadefoot Toads 65

Plains Spadefoot Toad (*Scaphiopus bombifrons*) 66

Eastern Spadefoot Toad (*Scaphiopus h. holbrookii*) 68

Family Bufonidae, True Toads 70

American Toad (*Bufo americanus*) 71

Great Plains Toad (*Bufo cognatus*) 74

Woodhouse's Toad (*Bufo woodhousei*) 76

Family Hylidae, Treefrogs, Chorus Frogs, and Cricket Frogs 79

Blanchard's Cricket Frog (*Acris crepitans blanchardi*) 80

Green Treefrog (*Hyla cinerea*) 82

Northern Spring Peeper (*Hyla c. crucifer*) 85

Gray Treefrogs (*Hyla versicolor* and *H. chrysoscelis*) 87

Illinois Chorus Frog (*Pseudacris streckeri illinoensis*) 90

Western Chorus Frog (*Pseudacris triseriata*) 92

Family Microhylidae, Narrow-mouthed Toads 94

Eastern Narrow-mouthed Toad (*Gastrophryne carolinensis*) 95

Great Plains Narrow-mouthed Toad (*Gastrophryne olivacea*) 97

Family Ranidae, True Frogs 99

Northern Crawfish Frog (*Rana areolata circulosa*) ---- 100

Plains Leopard Frog (*Rana blairi*) ---- 102

Bullfrog (*Rana catesbeiana*) ---- 104

Green Frog (*Rana clamitans*) ---- 106

Pickerel Frog (*Rana palustris*) ---- 108

Southern Leopard Frog (*Rana sphenocephala*) ---- 111

Wood Frog (*Rana sylvatica*) ---- 114

Amphibians of Possible Occurrence in Missouri ---- 116

Glossary ---- 117

Bibliography ---- 119

Index to Families, Common and Scientific Names ---- 128

INTRODUCTION

This is a book about the amphibians of Missouri. Ask the average person to name an amphibian, and he or she will probably answer, "a turtle." Of all the various vertebrate animals living today, the amphibians (toads, frogs, salamanders, and the tropical caecilians) are probably among the least known and the least understood.

There are close to 3,000 species of amphibians, which make up the Class Amphibia and have representatives living on all the continents except Antarctica. These animals have played a vital role in the evolution of the vertebrates (animals with backbones). The early amphibians were the first vertebrates to leave the security of their watery world and venture forth on land. These early amphibians evolved from a group of fresh water fish called "lobed-finned" fish. Some amphibians became established on land (if only during a part of their lives), and were able to advance to the point where they no longer had to return to swamps and marshes to breed and lay eggs. These animals became the first reptiles. Different groups of reptiles gave rise to both birds and mammals.

The study of amphibians and reptiles is called herpetology. This branch of zoology specifically treats both amphibians (salamanders, toads and frogs), and reptiles (turtles, lizards, snakes, crocodilians and the tuatara). A person devoted to this branch of science is called a herpetologist. The amphibians studied by herpetologists today are more than simply a link with the prehistoric past. Studying the natural history of these animals can help scientists understand the needs and relationships of complex animal communities, which can, in turn, help all of us gain a better understanding of our environment. Animals such as tadpoles and salamanders are useful as indicators of a changing environment. Studies by herpetologists help teach young people to appreciate and understand the natural biological systems of which we are all a part. Hopefully, in the years to come the job of trying to preserve our wildlife heritage will be shared by everyone.

Missouri truly has a rich amphibian fauna, with 48 kinds (species and subspecies) currently recognized. Because of the geographic location of Missouri, species of amphibians from northern, southern, eastern and western areas have been recorded here. A number of these species, however, have very limited distributions in Missouri. The caves, springs, and cold water streams of the beautiful Missouri Ozarks offer ideal habitats to many species of amphibians, and without such areas, a number of these animals would not be found here.

Living amphibians are placed in three major groups: salamanders (Order Caudata), toads and frogs (Order Anura), and caecilians (Order Apoda). The last group of amphibians are long, legless, worm-like animals from the tropics and are not treated in this book. Salamanders, toads, and frogs have moist skin with no scales; they require water or at least a damp environment in which to live. The majority of them must return to the water to reproduce and none are able to control their body temperature by internal means. Skin secretions of amphibians are somewhat toxic, and hands must be washed after touching them.

All Missouri amphibians lay eggs, either in the water or in moist areas. The eggs of toads and frogs develop into tadpoles which have gills that are covered by flaps of skin. The tadpoles of toads and frogs and the larvae of salamanders are extremely difficult to identify; the task of trying to describe them would be beyond the scope of this book. Line drawings of the typical tadpole and the two major types of salamander larvae are provided to familiarize the reader with their general appearances (Fig. 1).

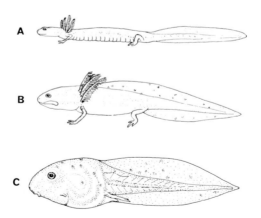

Fig. 1. Drawing of typical salamander larvae and tadpole. A. Stream-type larva with small gills and low tail fin. B. Pond-type larva with large gills and high tail fin. C. Tadpole.

Amphibian Classification

The Class Amphibia is divided into 3 orders:

Caudata _____ Salamanders
Apoda _____ Caecilians
Anura _____ Toads and Frogs

Each order is further divided into Families. For example some of the frogs of Missouri are placed in the following families:

Hylidae _____ treefrogs
Ranidae _____ true frogs

Families are composed of closely related groups called genera (singular, genus). An example would be the treefrogs (Family Hylidae), which consists of the following genera found in Missouri:

Acris _____ cricket frogs
Hyla _____ treefrogs
Pseudacris _____ chorus frogs

Final classification groups the even closer related members of each genus, the species. Thus, our Missouri treefrogs (genus *Hyla*) include the following species:

Hyla cinerea _____ green treefrog
Hyla crucifer _____ spring peeper
Hyla versicolor _____ gray treefrog

A subspecies name is added to a species name to indicate geographic variation within a species. For example two geographic variations of the chorus frog *(Pseudacris triseriata)* are the western chorus frog, *Pseudacris triseriata triseriata*, and the upland chorus frog, *Pseudacris triseriata feriarum*, both of which are found in Missouri.

Physiographic Provinces of Missouri

This information is furnished to familiarize the reader with the physical make-up of the state. These physical differences have a strong influence on what types of amphibians might occur in a particular section.

FIG. 2. Map of Missouri showing Physiographic Provinces. 1. Glaciated Province. 2. Osage Prairie. 3. Ozark Plateau. 4. Mississippi Lowlands.

Glaciated Province.—The physical features of this region reflect the southern-most movement and eventual retreat of the Kansan glacier, which took place about 400,000 years ago. The underlying rock of the area was ground up by the ice sheet, which caused the accumulation of thick deposits of gravel. The rolling hills and broad flat valleys seen in this area today were caused by the slow retreat of the glacier. To the east, along the Mississippi River, are large hills and limestone bluffs which were spared by the advance of the glacier. Average annual precipitation is 36 inches.

Some of the prairie species associated with this area are the Plains spadefoot toad *(Scaphiopus bombifrons)*, the plains leopard frog *(Rana blairi)*, and the northern crawfish frog *(Rana areolata circulosa)*. The majority of salamanders common to Missouri are missing from this area.

Osage Prairie.—Wide, flat prairies or gently rolling grassy hills typify this area. Average annual precipitation is 38 inches. Some of the western species listed in the above region, as well as the Woodhouse's toad *(Bufo woodhousei woodhousei)*, and the Great Plains narrow-mouthed toad *(Gastrophryne olivacea)*, are known from this area.

Ozarkian Plateau.—This area contains a large number of the salamanders, as well as many of the toads and frogs, found in the state. The rough terrain, clear streams, limestone bluffs, and cedar glades, as well as many springs and hundreds of caves give this area its unique character. A large part of this region is, or once was, a vast hardwood forest of oak, hickory, and maple. This province has the highest elevation in the state, Taum Sauk Mountain, 1,772 feet above sea level. Due to the poor soil and rough topography, agriculture has not taken as strong a hold on the area as it has in northern and western Missouri. Lumbering has been a major industry in the region, and large areas are now under the management of the National Forest Service. However, major sections of wooded areas recently have been cleared and seeded in grasses to furnish pasture for cattle and in time this may have a devastating effect on the flora and fauna of the Ozarks. The construction of dams and reservoirs in this area also has caused the destruction of many habitats, especially caves and springs. Average annual precipitation is 40 inches.

The Ozarks have several amphibians which are unique to the area: Ozark hellbender *(Cryptobranchus alleganiensis bishopi)*, gray-bellied salamander *(Eurycea multiplicata griseogaster)*, and grotto salamander *(Typhlotriton spelaeus)*.

Mississippi Lowlands.—The southeastern corner or "boot heel" of Missouri is a broad, flat alluvial flood plain of the Mississippi River. This is the lowest area in Missouri, averaging 325 feet above sea level. At one time the area was a vast cypress swamp, but due to extensive lumbering and drainage programs most of the area is now devoted to agriculture, especially cotton farming. Average annual precipitation is 46 inches. Even though the swamplands are nearly gone, a few amphibians typical of the southern United States are still present in a few areas of this province: the mole salamander (*Ambystoma talpoideum*), three-toed amphiuma (*Amphiuma tridactylum*), and the green treefrog (*Hyla cinerea*).

EXPLANATION OF FAMILY AND SPECIES ACCOUNTS

Family Accounts.—The families (12 in all) of the various amphibians native to Missouri are placed in the sequence used by Smith (1961) and Collins (1974). These accounts acquaint the reader with the general characteristics common to each family, and also list species which occur outside of Missouri. This information is furnished to give the reader an idea of the relationships and distributions of amphibians on a broader scale. An illustration of a typical example of each family is shown at the beginning of each family account.

Common and Scientific Names.—The common and scientific names used throughout this book are those currently accepted by most authorities. The common names follow Conant *et al.* (1956), or have been modified to conform to Conant (1975). The same is true for the scientific names, but if these names have had recent changes, a comment to that effect will be found in the *Remarks* section of the species accounts. I recommend that all persons, schools, museums, and zoos use the common names set down in this book to help standardize usage and prevent needless confusion in reading and conversation.

The genera found in each family are placed in alphabetical order and the species are placed in alphabetical order within each genus.

Description.—This first section in the species accounts furnishes characters to help identify each species, including general shape, a brief description of color and pattern, and when appropriate, a discussion of external characters that help separate the sexes of adults.

The size of each species is given in both metric and English units. Total length is given for salamanders (*i.e.*, length from the snout to the end of the tail). Sizes of toads and frogs are given in snout-vent length (*i.e.*, from the tip of the nose to the vent or anus). The majority of species lengths used here are those reported by Conant (1975).

Habits and Habitat.—Aspects of the natural history of each species are discussed when known. This includes habitat preferences, daily and seasonal activity, food, and specific behavioral traits.

Breeding.—The reproductive biology of Missouri amphibians is discussed in this section. This includes courtship, mating, egg laying, nesting, hatching and development of larvae and young. Also included is the duration of the breeding season, and, in the case of toads and frogs, a description of their breeding calls. The bulk of this information was obtained from works by Bishop (1947), Wright and Wright (1949), Smith (1961), Barbour (1971), Collins (1974), and Conant (1975). The rest was gleaned from published papers in various journals.

Remarks.—This section is placed in a species account when special information is offered, such as recommendations for conservation efforts, hybridization, and explanation of taxonomic problems.

Distribution and Maps.—At the end of each species account is a brief description of the range of the species in Missouri. Also included is a map of Missouri which shows both the presumed range, shown by shading, and the known range, shown by large dots in the counties. Subspecies are differentiated on the maps by using different types of shading. Sections of the state where subspecies are thought to intergrade are shown by overlapping of shading.

The solid circles represent county records based on preserved animals housed in herpetological collections of museums or universities. Open circles represent amphibians observed in the field by me, or other investigators, but not collected. Preserved amphibian specimens were examined and/or county records were gathered from the following institutions:

St. Louis Museum of Science and Natural History
University of Missouri, Columbia
Northwest Missouri State University, Maryville
Northeast Missouri State University, Kirksville
Culver-Stockton College, Canton, Mo.
Southern Illinois University, Carbondale
Field Museum of Natural History, Chicago, Ill.
Chicago Academy of Science
Illinois Natural History Survey, Urbana
University of Illinois Natural History Museum, Urbana
University of Kansas, Museum of Natural History, Lawrence
Milwaukee Public Museum
National Museum of Natural History, Smithsonian Institution
American Museum of Natural History, New York
University of Michigan Museum of Zoology, Ann Arbor

For those readers who wish to learn about the distribution of amphibians outside the confines of Missouri, I suggest referring to *A Field Guide of Reptiles and Amphibians of Eastern and Central North America*, by Roger Conant (1975).

Photographs and Illustrations.—Photographs are intended to show each animal in a natural setting, but at the same time have them shown clearly. All species accounts have at least one photograph, although in several accounts a subspecies photograph is also included. Additional photographs, showing a calling male toad or frog, or a pair in amplexus are furnished in a few accounts. All photographs were taken, and all line drawings were rendered, by the author.

CHECKLIST OF MISSOURI AMPHIBIANS

CLASS AMPHIBIA
Order Caudata—Salamanders

Family Cryptobranchidae—Giant Salamanders
   Hellbender _____ *Cryptobranchus alleganiensis alleganiensis*
(Daudin)
   Ozark Hellbender _____ *Cryptobranchus alleganiensis bishopi*
Grobman
Family Sirenidae—Sirens
   Western Lesser Siren _____ *Siren intermedia nettingi* Goin
Family Ambystomatidae—Mole Salamanders
   Ringed Salamander _____ *Ambystoma annulatum* Cope
   Spotted Salamander _____ *Ambystoma maculatum* (Shaw)
   Marbled Salamander _____ *Ambystoma opacum* (Gravenhorst)
   Mole Salamander _____ *Ambystoma talpoideum* (Holbrook)
   Small-mouthed Salamander _____ *Ambystoma texanum* (Matthes)
   Eastern Tiger Salamander _____ *Ambystoma tigrinum tigrinum*
(Green)
Family Salamandridae—Newts
   Central Newt _____ *Notophthalmus viridescens louisianensis*
Wolterstorff
Family Amphiumidae—Amphiumas
   Three-toed Amphiuma _____ *Amphiuma tridactylum* Cuvier
Family Plethodontidae—Lungless Salamanders
   Long-tailed Salamander _____ *Eurycea longicauda longicauda*
(Green)
   Dark-sided Salamander _____ *Eurycea longicauda melanopleura*
(Cope)
   Cave Salamander _____ *Eurycea lucifuga* Rafinesque
   Gray-bellied Salamander _____ *Eurycea multiplicata griseogaster*
Moore & Hughes
   Oklahoma Salamander _____ *Eurycea tynerensis* Moore & Hughes
   Four-toed Salamander _____ *Hemidactylium scutatum* (Schlegel)
   Ozark Red-backed Salamander *Plethodon dorsails angusticlavius*
Grobman
   Slimy Salamander _____ *Plethodon glutinosus glutinosus* (Green)
   Southern Red-backed Salamander _____ *Plethodon serratus*
Grobman
   Grotto Salamander _____ *Typhlotriton spelaeus* Stejneger
Family Proteidae—Mudpuppy and Waterdogs
   Red River Waterdog ____ *Necturus maculosus louisanensis* Viosca
   Mudpuppy _____ *Necturus maculosus maculosus* (Rafinesque)
Order Anura—Toads and Frogs
Family Pelobatidae—Spadefoot Toads

Plains Spadefoot Toad _____ *Scaphiopus bombifrons* (Cope)
Eastern Spadefoot Toad _____ *Scaphiopus holbrookii holbrookii* (Harlan)

Family Bufonidae—True Toads
American Toad _____ *Bufo americanus americanus* Holbrook
Dwarf American Toad _____ *Bufo americanus charlesmithi* Bragg
Great Plains Toad _____ *Bufo cognatus* Say
Fowler's Toad _____ *Bufo woodhousei fowleri* Hinckley
Woodhouse's Toad _____ *Bufo woodhousei woodhousei* Girard

Family Hylidae—Cricket, Chorus & Treefrogs
Blanchard's Cricket Frog _____ *Acris crepitans blanchardi* Harper
Cope's Gray Treefrog _____ *Hyla chrysoscelis* Cope
Green Treefrog _____ *Hyla cinerea* (Schneider)
Northern Spring Peeper _____ *Hyla crucifer crucifer* Wied
Eastern Gray Treefrog _____ *Hyla versicolor* Le Conte
Illinois Chorus Frog _____ *Pseudacris streckeri illinoensis* Smith
Upland Chorus Frog _____ *Pseudacris triseriata feriarum* (Baird)
Western Chorus Frog _____ *Pseudacris triseriata triseriata* (Wied)

Family Microhylidae—Narrow-mouthed Toads
Eastern Narrow-mouthed Toad _____ *Gastrophryne carolinensis* (Holbrook)
Great Plains Narrow-mouthed Toad _____ *Gastrophryne olivacea* (Hallowell)

Family Ranidae—True Frogs
Northern Crawfish Frog _____ *Rana areolata circulosa* Rice & Davis
Plains Leopard Frog _____ *Rana blairi* Mecham, Littlejohn, Oldham, Brown & Brown
Bullfrog _____ *Rana catesbeiana* Shaw
Bronze Frog _____ *Rana clamitans clamitans* Latreille
Green Frog _____ *Rana clamitans melanota* (Rafinesque)
Pickerel Frog _____ *Rana palustris* Le Conte
Southern Leopard Frog _____ *Rana sphenocephala* Cope
Wood Frog _____ *Rana sylvatica* Le Conte

KEYS TO THE AMPHIBIANS OF MISSOURI
HOW TO USE THE KEYS

The illustrated keys which follow are furnished to help the reader identify all *adult* amphibians known to occur in Missouri. The keys have been designed to identify living animals, not preserved specimens. Tadpoles, larvae, and young cannot be identified with these keys.

Keys used to identify species are a series of numbered couplets which furnish a choice of characteristics (*a* and *b*) in each couplet. By selecting the description which best fits the amphibian being identified, and by continuing to refer to each couplet numbered at the end of each proper characteristic, the reader eventually is directed to a couplet which ends in the name of the animal. Illustrations of important characteristics are furnished and labelled with the couplet number with which they correspond. The page number, in parentheses at the end of each species name, refers to the page where the species account begins. Some of the external features used to identify salamanders and frogs are shown in Fig. 3.

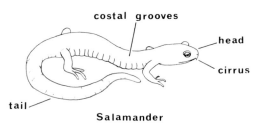

Salamander

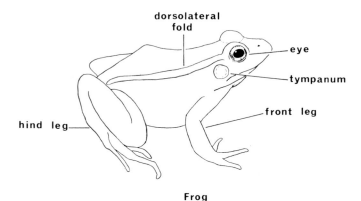

Frog

FIG. 3. Generalized drawing of a typical Salamander and Frog.

Key to the Adult Salamanders of Missouri

1a. Body eel-like; dark gray to brown or black; permanently aquatic; with or without gills; legs reduced or hind legs absent _____ 2

1b. Body not eel-like; legs well developed; with or without gills _____ 3

2a. Only front legs present; with gills; tail compressed vertically; color dull brown _____ Western Lesser Siren, *Siren intermedia nettingi* (Fig. 4, p. 22).

2b. Two pairs of tiny legs, with 3 toes on each leg; tail not compressed; color dark gray-brown to black; an opening present on either side of the rear of the head; no gills _____ Three-toed Amphiuma, *Amphiuma tridactylum* (Fig. 4, p. 42).

3a. Both front and hind legs with 4 toes _____ 4

3b. Front legs with 4 toes; hind legs with 5 toes _____ 5

4a. Large feathery gills; tail compressed; color tan to dull gray-brown; numerous dusky or dark spots over dorsum and tail _____ Mudpuppy and Waterdog, *Necturus maculosus* (Fig. 4, p. 63).

4b. No gills; tail rounded and with constriction at base; white belly with black spots _____ Four-toed salamander, *Hemidactylium scutatum* (p. 52).

5a. Costal grooves absent _____ 6

5b. Costal grooves present _____ 7

6a. Size 70-100 mm (2⅞-4 inches); olive-brown dorsum with two rows of tiny red spots; belly yellow with numerous black spots; found in ponds _____ Central Newt, *Notophthalmus viridescens louisianensis* (p. 38).

6b. Size 29.3-51 cm (11½-20 inches); permanently aquatic; no gills; head and body flattened; longitudinal wrinkles over body and tail; dorsum gray to reddish brown, belly grayish-brown; found in rivers _____ Hellbender, *Cryptobranchus alleganiensis* (Fig. 4, p. 19).

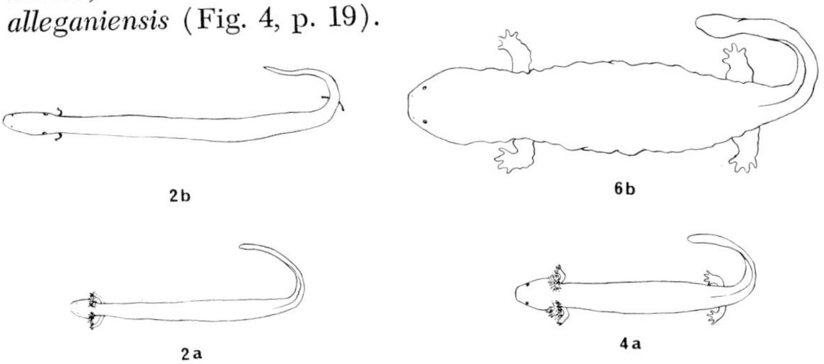

Fig. 4. Outline drawing of aquatic salamanders: Siren (2a); Three-toed Amphiuma (2b); Mudpuppy (4a); and Hellbender (6b).

7a. Tail heavy, same length as body or shorter; general ground color dark brown to black; no naso-labial grooves _____ 8

7b. Tail slender, as long or longer than body; naso-labial groove present _____ 13

8a. Tail as long as head and body length; dorsum with grayish flecks or crossbands; costal grooves 14-15 _____ 9

8b. Tail as long as or shorter than head and body length; dorsum with flecks, round spots, cross bars, or large blotches; costal grooves 10-15 _____ 10

9a. Body and tail plain or with numerous gray flecks; no rings. _____ Small-mouthed Salamander, *Ambystoma texanum* (p. 33).

9b. Narrow transverse white or yellowish rings from head to tip of tail _____ Ringed Salamander, *Ambystoma annulatum* (p. 25).

10a. Transverse gray or silvery bars; costal grooves 11-12 _____ Marbled Salamander, *Ambystoma opacum* (p. 29).

10b. No transverse bars; uniform dark color or with spots or blotches; costal grooves 10-15 _____ 11

11a. With or without faded lichen-like gray flecks; costal grooves 10-11 _____ Mole Salamander, *Ambystoma talpoideum* (p. 31).

11b. Yellow spots or large yellowish blotches over body and tail; costal grooves 11-15 _____ 12

12a. Dorsum with two rows of round, yellow spots; numerous white flecks on sides of body; costal grooves 11-12 _____ Spotted Salamander, *Ambystoma maculatum* (p. 27).

12b. Numerous olive-brown or yellowish irregular blotches; no white flecks on sides of body; costal grooves 12-15 _____ Eastern Tiger Salamander, *Ambystoma tigrinum tigrinum* (p. 35).

13a. Body and tail long and slender; with or without gills; costal grooves 19-20 _____ 14

13b. Tail rounded or slightly compressed; no gills; costal grooves 14-20 _____ 15

14a. Tail fin present; gills present (neotenic); 2 rows of light spots along sides; belly pale and without markings; no row of chevrons along midline of dorsum _____ Oklahoma Salamander, *Eurycea tynerensis* (p. 51).

14b. Gills present or absent; one row of light spots along side; belly gray, may have some yellow color; row of chevrons along midline of dorsum _____ Gray-bellied Salamander, *Eurycea multiplicata griseogaster* (p. 49).

15a. Color brown or black; flecks of white or dorsal stripe present _____ 16

15b. Color tan, yellow, or orange; with or without dark spots ____ 17

16a. Color jet black; with numerous white or yellowish flecks over dorsum of head, body, and tail; no dorsal stripe; belly plain gray; costal grooves 14-15 _____ Slimy Salamander, *Plethodon glutinosus glutinosus* (p. 56).

16b. Color brown; dorsum of body and tail with orange or red stripe; belly with white and black mottling _____ 18

17a. Light tan color; no markings; eyes sometimes covered over with skin; tail rounded; costal grooves 16-19; found deep inside caves only _____ Grotto Salamander, *Typhlotriton spelaes* (p. 60).

17b. Color greenish-yellow, orange, or red-orange; dark spots on head and body; spots or bars on tail, tail long and slender _____ 19

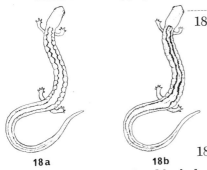

18a. Dorsal stripe uniform in width, not widest at hind legs; stripe edges serrated or sawtoothed, points of serrations corresponding to costal grooves; costal grooves 18-19 (Fig. 5.) _____ Southern Red-backed Salamander, *Plethodon serratus* (p. 58).

18b. Dorsal stripe narrow and broken or lobed; stripe widest at hind legs; costal grooves 17-19 (Fig. 5.) _____ Ozark

18a   **18b**
Fig. 5. Dorsal view of Red-backed Salamanders: Southern (18a); Ozark (18b).

Red-backed Salamander, *Plethodon dorsalis angusticlavius* (p. 54).

19a. General color greenish-yellow, yellow to orange-yellow; dark irregular spots on dorsum; dark markings on tail in the form of bars; or fused to form a dark lateral line on body and tail _____ Long-tailed and Dark-sided Salamander, *Eurycea longicauda* (p. 45).

19b. General color bright orange or red-orange; numerous small black spots on body and tail; no stripe on side of body or tail _____ Cave Salamander, *Eurycea lucifuga* (p. 47).

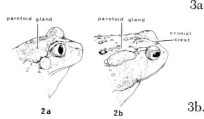

2a   2b

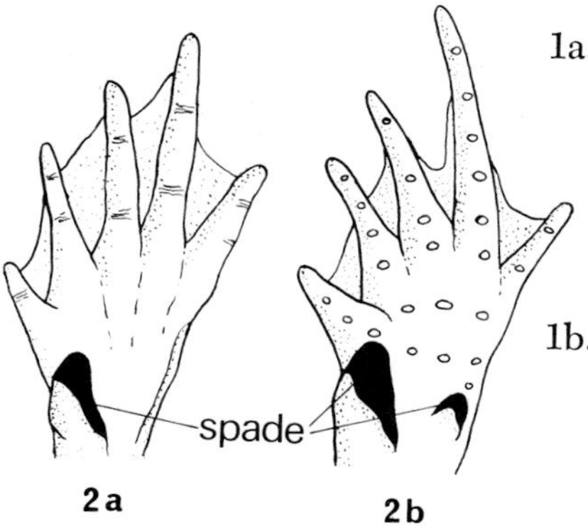

FIG. 6. Underside of hind feet of Spadefoot Toad (2a) and true Toad (2b).

1a. One or two large spades on heel of each hind foot (Fig. 6); numerous warts; little or no webbing between toes of hind feet; paratoid glands behind eyes; skin relatively dry -- 2

1b. No spades on heel of hind feet; skin generally wartless; no parotoid glands behind eyes; weak to strongly webbed toes on hind feet; skin relatively moist ---------- 6

2a. Paratoid glands small and round; eye with vertical pupil (Fig. 7); no bony cranial crest on head; only one spade per hind foot (Fig. 6); scattered warts ------------------------------------ 3

2b. Parotoid glands large; eye with horizontal pupil (Fig. 6); bony cranial crest on head; one large and one small spade per hind foot (Fig. 6); numerous warts ------------------------------- 4

with horizontal pupil (Fig. 7); bony cranial crest on head; one large and one small spade per hind foot (Fig. 6); numerous warts -- 4

parotoid gland   parotoid gland

cranial crest

2a   2b

FIG. 7. Side view of heads of Spadefoot Toad (2a) and true Toad (2b).

3a. Pronounced boss between eyes; spade on hind feet short and rounded; general color tan to greenish-tan; warts may be red ---------- Plains Spadefoot Toad, *Scaphiopus bombifrons* (p. 66).

3b. No boss between eyes; spade elongated and sickle-shaped; general color dull yellow, tan or brown; 2 or 4 yellowish longitudinal lines on dorsum; warts may be orange ----------
Eastern Spadefoot Toad, *Scaphiopus holbrookii holbrookii* (p. 68).

4a. Parotoid glands oblong and connected to cranial crest; general color light gray to greenish gray; 3 or more warts per large dorsal spot; belly plain white, or with one dark spot on chest
--- 5

4b. Parotoid glands kidney-shaped, either separate from cranial crest or connected with a short spur; general coloration light brown to reddish brown; 3 or less warts per large dorsal spot; chest spotted with dusky markings or having only a few dark spots ---------- American Toad and Dwarf American Toad, *Bufo americanus* (p. 71).

5a. Raised boss between eyes; general color creamy white to light greenish-tan; dorsal blotches greenish-brown bordered by white, large and paired _____ Great Plains Toad, *Bufo cognatus* (p. 74).

5b. No raised boss between eyes; general color gray to grayish-brown; dorsal spots brown to black; usually with a single chest spot _____ Woodhouse's and Fowler's Toad, *Bufo woodhousei* (p. 76).

6a. Tips of toes on front and hind feet expanded to form adhesive toe pads, which may be very small or large; if toe pads not present, with a V-shaped marking or small triangle between eyes; no dorsolateral fold _____ 7

6b. Tips of toes on front and hind feet without adhesive toe pads; no V-shaped marking or small triangle between eyes; with or without dorsolateral fold; if without dorsolateral fold may have a transverse fold of skin behind head _____ 12

7a. Tips of toes with adhesive toe pads; no V-shaped or small triangular marking between eyes _____ 8

7b. Tips of toes without adhesive toe pads; V-shaped or small triangular marking between eyes _____ 9

8a. Toe pads small; dorsal markings in the form of long stripes or lines of spots _____ Upland and Western Chorus Frogs, *Pseudacris triseriata* (p. 92).

8b. Toe pads medium to large size _____ 10

9a. V-shaped marking between eyes; front legs large and muscular; no alternating light and dark bars on upper lip; a dark spot below each eye; no black stripe along inner thighs _____ Illinois Chorus Frog, *Pseudacris streckeri illinoensis* (p. 90).

9b. Dark triangle-shaped marking between eyes; front legs small and not muscular; no dark spot below each eye; alternating light and dark bars on upper lip; rough-edged black stripe along each inner thigh _____ Blanchard's Cricket Frog, *Acris crepitans blanchardi* (p. 80).

10a. Toe pads prominent; general color yellow-green to emerald green; yellow line extending from snout to about midway to hind legs; dorsum may have a few small white or golden spots _____ Green Treefrog, *Hyla cinerea* (p. 82).

10b. Toe pads small to prominent; with or without white spot below eyes; color gray, tan or greenish-gray; no yellow lateral line _____ 11

11a. Toe pads small; no white spot below eyes; color pinkish-tan to grayish-tan; dark line between eyes; dorsal marking in the form of an X; no bright orange-yellow color on underside of thighs _____ Northern Spring Peeper, *Hyla crucifer crucifer* (p. 85).

11b. Toe pads prominent; large white spot below eyes; general color may be light gray to greenish-gray, to brown; dark irregular blotches on dorsum; no dark line between eyes; underside of thighs bright orange-yellow .... Cope's and Eastern Gray Treefrogs, *Hyla chrysoscelis* and *H. versicolor* (p. 87).

12a. Head small (less than ¼ snout-vent length); transverse fold of skin behind head; no tympanum; no dorsolateral folds 13

12b. Head large (greater than ¼ snout-vent length); no transverse fold of skin behind head; tympanum prominent; with or without dorsolateral folds _____ 14

13a. Color uniform dark brown, two wide light stripes along each side of dorsum; belly heavily marked with dark pigment .... Eastern Narrow-mouthed Toad, *Gastrophryne carolinensis* (p. 95).

13b. Color uniform gray to olive-tan; no markings or stripes on dorsum; belly light gray or creamy-yellow without mottling .... Great Plains Narrow-mouthed Toad, *Gastrophryne olivacea* (p. 97).

14a. With distinct dorsolateral folds; general color pinkish-tan, or grayish-brown; large dark marking on sides of head extending from snout through eye and nearly to front legs; no prominent dorsal markings .... Wood Frog, *Rana sylvatica* (p. 114).

14b. With or without dorsolateral folds; general color tan, brown, or greenish-brown; no large dark markings on sides of head; with or without large dorsal spots or blotches 15

15a. With or without dorsolateral folds; no light line along upper lip; tympanum same size or larger than eye; few and indistinct dorsal markings _____ 16

15b. Dorsolateral folds prominent; with distinct dorsal spots or blotches; with or without light line along upper lip; tympanum same size as eye _____ 17

16a. No dorsolateral folds; prominent tympanal fold of skin from eye to shoulder; upper lip green; dorsal spots usually obscured if present .... Bullfrog, *Rana catesbeiana* (p. 104).

16b. Dorsolateral folds extending halfway to hind legs; tympanal fold of skin from eye to shoulder not prominent; head greenish; with a few small dorsal spots .... Green Frog and Bronze Frog, *Rana clamitans* (p. 106).

17a. No light line on upper lip; dorsal spots numerous and closely set, interspaced with reticulations of dark brown or black .... Northern Crawfish Frog, *Rana areolata circulosa* (p. 100).

17b. Light line on upper lip; dorsal spots scattered or in two distinct rows down the dorsum, not interspaced with reticulations of dark brown or black _____ 18

18a. Dorsal spots squarish or rectangular, and set in two longitudinal rows (Fig. 8); underside of hind legs yellow .... Pickerel Frog, *Rana palustris* (p. 108).

18b. Dorsal spots rounded or oblong; no bright yellow color on underside of hind legs 19

19a. Snout rounded; dorsal spots small, round, and extending to near hind legs; general color tan to light brown, no green color on dorsum; dorsolateral folds broken, posterior section displaced toward midline (Fig. 8) .... Plains Leopard Frog, *Rana blairi* (p. 102).

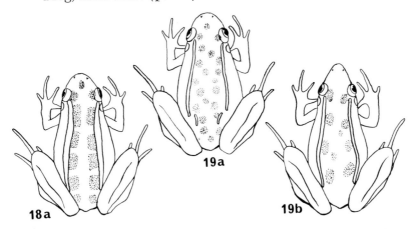

FIG. 8. Dorsal view of Pickerel Frog (18a); Plains Leopard Frog (19a); and Southern Leopard Frog (19b).

19b. Snout pointed; dorsal spots small to medium in size, rounded and/or oblong and well spaced; usually some green color on dorsum; dorsolateral fold continuous, but if broken near hind legs, broken section not medially displaced (Fig. 8) .... Southern Leopard Frog, *Rana sphenocephala* (p. 111).

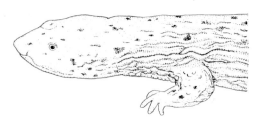

Fig. 9. Hellbender, *Cryptobranchus alleganiensis.*

Family Cryptobranchidae
GIANT SALAMANDERS

This family contains two genera, *Andrias* and *Cryptobranchus.* *Andrias* is strictly Asiatic, with two living forms, the Chinese and Japanese giant salamanders (*A. davidens* and *A. japonicus,* respectively). The Japanese giant salamander is the largest living amphibian in the world, and has been reported up to five feet in length.

The other genus, *Cryptobranchus,* is restricted to the United States. Two subspecies, the hellbender, *C. a. alleganiensis,* and the Ozark hellbender, *C. a. bishopi,* are recognized. Although primarily an eastern species, the hellbender is common in Missouri. The Ozark hellbender is restricted to southern Missouri and a small part of northern Arkansas. Missouri is the only state that contains both geographic varieties.

All members of this family are permanently aquatic (paedogenetic) salamanders.

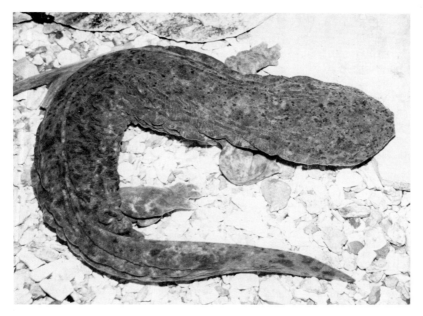

FIG. 10. Adult Ozark Hellbender, *Cryptobranchus alleganiensis bishopi.*

HELLBENDER

Cryptobranchus alleganiensis (Daudin)

Description.—A large aquatic salamander. Its head is large but flat, with very small, lidless, eyes. Sides of body have soft, pronounced folds of skin with large flaps of skin on front and hind limbs. The tail is flattened and rudder-like. A single gill opening is usually present on one side of the head. Coloration varies from reddish-brown to dull gray-brown. Some dark markings occur on the back and tail, but they do not make up a distinct pattern. The belly is a uniform dark tan or gray-brown, and is lighter in color than the rest of the body.

The hellbender ranges in total length from 29.3-51 cm (11½-20 inches). The record size is 74 cm (29 inches; Conant, 1975).

Habits and Habitat.—The hellbender is well suited for an aquatic existence. Its flat head and streamlined shape reduce water resistance. This salamander makes its home under flat rocks in large permanent streams and rivers. It is a slow swimmer, and often moves by walking along the bottom. It is normally a solitary animal, and usually only one will be found at a time hiding under a rock (Nickerson and Mays, 1973).

In a recent study in Missouri (Nickerson and Mays, 1973), hellbenders were found to feed mainly on crawfish although other aquatic animals were occasionally eaten. I have found that captive hellbenders will eat crawfish, minnows, and earthworms.

Breeding.—Hellbenders breed in the fall (late September to November) and are the only salamanders in Missouri which fertilize their eggs externally. Between 250-400 eggs (each about 6 mm in diameter) are deposited under a flat rock. The eggs are laid in long strands, like a string of beads, and will hatch out in six to eight weeks. The larvae take over two years to lose their gills and take on adult characteristics.

Subspecies.—There are two subspecies of hellbender in Missouri. The Ozark hellbender, *Cryptobranchus alleganiensis bishopi* Grobman, is found in southeast Missouri. One of the characteristics which distinguishes the two forms is the presence of black or dusky markings over a large part of the chin of *C. a. bishopi,* which is usually lacking in the other subspecies, *C. a. alleganiensis.* Also, the dark brown markings on the back are more numerous on the Ozark hellbender. Nickerson and Mays (1973) found that the Ozark hellbender is smaller and weighs less (largest Missouri specimen 53.5 cm) than *C. a. alleganiensis.*

Remarks.—Hellbenders are often caught by fishermen in streams and rivers of southern Missouri, and are thought to be dangerous, poisonous, and deadly. None of this is true. The hellbender is a harmless amphibian which seldom, if ever, attempts to bite, and if caught, should never be killed.

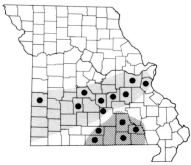

Missouri Distribution.—The hellbender is restricted to the Ozark Plateau in rivers which drain into the Missouri-Mississippi River system. The Ozark hellbender is found in the Black River system and the North Fork of the White River (hatching).

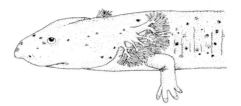

Fig. 11. Western Lesser Siren, *Siren intermedia nettingi.*

FAMILY SIRENIDAE
SIRENS AND LESSER SIRENS

This family of completely aquatic salamanders is restricted to North America. There are only three species represented by two genera: *Siren* (two species) and *Pseudobranchus* (one species). All members of this family have external gills, are somewhat eel-like in appearance, and have only front legs. The dwarf sirens, *Pseudobranchus,* are small slender salamanders found in the extreme southeastern United States. The lesser siren and the greater siren (genus *Siren*) are much larger than *Pseudobranchus,* and are found throughout the southeast and south central United States and eastern Mexico. The greater siren, *Siren lacertina,* is one of the longest salamanders in the United States with a maximum length of over 90 cm (3 feet). In Missouri the family is represented by the western lesser siren, *Siren intermedia nettingi.*

FIG. 12. Sub-adult Western Lesser Siren, *Siren intermedia nettingi.*

WESTERN LESSER SIREN
Siren intermedia nettingi Goin

Description.—Characterized by external gills, small eyes, lack of hind legs, and small front legs with four toes. The general shape of this animal is eel-like. The three pairs of external gills are red or grayish-red in color and have a bushy appearance. Coloration varies from dark gray to brown to almost black. The belly is lighter than the back. Tiny dark brown or black flecks or spots are usually scattered over the back. Costal grooves vary from 34-36. There is no apparent external difference between the two sexes except that males are larger than females.

Adult western lesser sirens range in length from 18-40.7 cm (7-16 inches). The record length is 50.2 cm (19¾ inches; Conant, 1975).

Habits and Habitat.—This completely aquatic salamander is found in ditches, ponds, sloughs, and swamps. By day it remains hidden under clumps of aquatic plants and submerged roots or branches, but becomes active at night to search for food. Its diet includes small crawfish, aquatic insects, snails and worms.

Western lesser sirens are known to produce two kinds of sounds, both of which may be used as means of communication between individuals. These include clicking sounds made by an individual when approached by another, and a "yelp" sound made when captured (Gehlbach and Walker, 1970; Conant, 1975).

If the pond or slough in which a western lesser siren lives begins to dry up, it will burrow into the bottom mud. Then as the mud begins to dry out, the siren's skin glands produce a parchment-like cocoon which covers the entire body except the head. This covering protects the salamander from drying out, and allows it to aestivate many months until rains again flood the pond (Gehlbach *et al.,* 1973; Conant, 1975).

Breeding.—Breeding behavior has not been observed in this species. In the spring each female lays up to 200 eggs in a small pocket in the bottom mud of a pond or ditch. The young at hatching are about 11 mm (⅜ inch) in total length. Maturity is reached after two years of development (Martof, 1973).

Remarks.—Sirens produce a large amount of slime on their skin making them very difficult to handle. Add to this the ability to wiggle and squirm, and handling is next to impossible. From what is currently known, these salamanders do not bite and are completely harmless to humans.

Missouri Distribution.—The western lesser siren has been collected in the extreme eastern portion of the Ozark Plateau and in the Mississippi River lowlands.

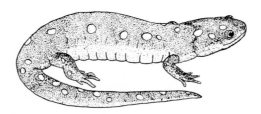

Fig. 13. A typical Mole Salamander, *Ambystoma maculatum*.

FAMILY AMBYSTOMATIDAE
MOLE SALAMANDERS

Members of this family (32 species in 4 genera) are found throughout most of the United States and parts of Canada and Mexico. The genus *Ambystoma* includes the majority of species and is the only genus of this family found in Missouri. There are six species of *Ambystoma* in our state.

The majority of Missouri species breed in early spring, courting and depositing their eggs in shallow ponds. Exceptions to this breeding behavior are discussed in the species accounts. The gilled larvae usually transform from aquatic to land forms in late summer, but some may spend the winter as larvae and transform the next summer.

In Missouri, adult *Ambystoma* spend most of their time burrowing in the soil or under logs and rocks. They may be seen wandering about at night, especially after a heavy rain.

FIG. 14. Adult Ringed Salamander, *Ambystoma annulatum*.

RINGED SALAMANDER
Ambystoma annulatum Cope

Description.—A slender and elongated salamander, usually with 15 costal grooves (J. D. Anderson, 1965). The head and neck are somewhat elongated compared to other members of the genus. The dorsum ground color ranges from a dark brown to black; the belly is normally a buff yellow. A series of pale rings usually go completely over the back, but may be broken at the midline. The rings never completely encircle the body. Ring color may vary from a dull white to yellow.

Adults range in length from 140-180 mm (5½-7 inches). The record length is 235 mm (9¼ inches; Conant, 1975).

Habits and Habitat.—Because of the secretive nature of this salamander, little is known about its habits. The ringed salamander probably lives much like other members of the genus: hiding under logs and rocks, or burrowing in the soil, seldom venturing into the open, and preferring heavily forested areas. Its food habits have not been studied in Missouri, but food probably includes earthworms, insects, and land snails.

Breeding.—The ringed salamander breeds in the fall, usually between September and November. They are stimulated by heavy rains and cool temperatures to travel by night to breeding ponds where they congregate by the hundreds. The males arrive at the breeding ponds before the females and can be distinguished by their swollen cloacas. The eggs are fertilized internally, with courtship and egg laying taking place in shallow water. Breeding may last only a few days after which the salamanders begin to move away from the ponds (J. D. Anderson, 1965). Little is known about development of the larvae.

Remarks.—This species has been listed as "status undetermined" by the Missouri Department of Conservation in the *Rare and Endangered Fauna of Missouri* (1972). Because of its wide range in

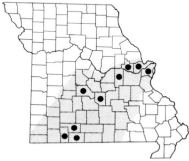

Missouri, and the large numbers that may be observed during the breeding season, this species may not be endangered. However, because of its vulnerability during fall breeding aggregations, and since it may be sought after by many collectors, I recommend that the ringed salamander be protected from all forms of collecting during the breeding season.

Missouri Distribution.—This salamander occurs throughout most of the forested Ozark Plateau.

Fig. 15. Adult Spotted Salamander, *Ambystoma maculatum*.

Spotted Salamander
Ambystoma maculatum (Shaw)

Description.—Dorsum ground color slate black, belly dark gray. Two irregular rows of rounded yellow spots from the head onto the tail. Several spots on the head may be bright orange-yellow. Sides of head, neck and body usually with small white flecks. Several specimens collected from Missouri lack most or all yellow spots.

Adult spotted salamanders range in length from 150-200 mm (6-7¾ inches). The record length is 240 mm (9 inches; Conant, 1975).

Habits and Habitat.—This species can be found in damp hardwood forests in the vicinity of shallow ponds, usually hidden under logs or rocks, inside piles of dead leaves, or burrowed in the soil. They venture forth at night in search of worms, insects, spiders, and land snails, and are often seen crossing roads on warm rainy nights.

Breeding.—The spotted salamander is an early spring breeder. During the first warm rains in late February or early March they congregate in shallow woodland ponds to court and lay eggs. As with all members of the family, the eggs are fertilized internally. During courtship two or more salamanders go through a series of movements somewhat like a nuptial dance. After this the male releases a packet of sperm (spermatophore) which is picked up by the cloaca of the female. Eggs are laid in a mass on submerged branchs or aquatic plants. The egg mass may contain from a dozen

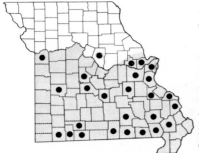

to over 250 eggs (Bishop, 1943). The gilled larvae hatch out in about a month and remain in the water until the end of the summer, at which time they begin adult life on land. Individuals may return to the same pond to breed year after year. Some larvae may over-winter in the pond and metamorphose during the next summer.

Missouri Distribution.—The spotted salamander is found throughout Missouri, except the northern third of the state.

Fig. 16. Adult Marbled Salamander, *Ambystoma opacum.*

MARBLED SALAMANDER
Ambystoma opacum (Gravenhorst)

Description.—This small, stout salamander has silvery saddle-shaped markings on its body from head to tail. These crossbands vary in shape and also in color from silver-white to gray. The back is generally shiny jet black, while the belly is plain black. Sex of an adult marbled salamander is distinguished by the color of the crossbands: on males they are white to silver, while on females they are dull gray. The average adult length of this species is 90-115 mm (3½-4½ inches). The record length is 127 mm (5 inches; Conant, 1975).

Habits and Habitat.—The marbled salamander is secretive, spending most of its time under rocks, logs, or forest debris. It prefers forested areas, but also may be found in open sandy woods and on dry rocky hillsides. Food probably consists of insects, worms, slugs, and other invertebrates found under rocks or logs.

Breeding.—In this species, courtship and fertilization of eggs takes place on land (most other members breed in ponds or ditches), and usually takes place in the fall. Fertilization is internal and the female may lay from 50-200 eggs (Bishop, 1943). The female stays with the eggs until autumn rains raise the water level of the ponds, covering the eggs. The larvae hatch and develop in the water. Metamorphosis takes place the following summer.

Remarks.—In parts of its range in Missouri, the marbled salamander becomes conspicuous as autumn breeding activities begin. This species would benefit from protection during its breeding season. Heavy collecting should be avoided during this critical period of its life cycle.

Missouri Distribution.—The marbled salamander is known to occur in the Mississippi River lowlands and the adjacent Ozark Plateau. However, it may also occur through much of the southeastern half of Missouri.

FIG. 17. Adult Mole Salamander, *Ambystoma talpoideum*.

MOLE SALAMANDER
Ambystoma talpoideum (Holbrook)

Description.—A salamander with seemingly over-large head, small legs and small tail. Costal grooves number 10-11. Coloration is usually dull gray or brown, and sometimes there are whitish or light gray flecks over most of the tail. Total length of adults range from 80-100 mm (3-4 inches). The record length is 122 (4 13/16 inches; Conant, 1975).

Habits and Habitat.—The natural history of the mole salamander is similar to that of the marbled salamander. It lives under rocks or rotten logs in swamps and deep forests, and is apt to dig down in burrows well into the ground. These amphibians are seldom encountered since they rarely venture above ground. However, they do become active on the surface during the breeding season.

Breeding.—No study of the breeding habits of this species has been carried out in Missouri. Smith (1961) reported that this species may be an autumn breeder in Illinois, and this may also be true for the populations in Missouri. Data from other areas indicate that leaf-littered woodland ponds or pools in swamps are utilized for breeding. Fertilization is internal and a female lays from 10-40 eggs in a loose cluster. The larval stage lasts from three to four months (Smith, 1961). Shoop (1964) reported that mole salamander larvae may live in crawfish burrows.

Remarks.—Because of its limited range in Missouri, the mole salamander should be listed as a threatened animal in this state.

Missouri Distribution.—The mole salamander was first reported in Missouri by Easterla (1967). It is restricted to the Mississippi River lowlands where it has been found in several locations.

Fig. 18. Adult Small-mouthed Salamander, *Ambystoma texanum*.

SMALL-MOUTHED SALAMANDER
Ambystoma texanum (Matthes)

Description.—The small-mouthed salamander is of moderate size, has a small head and mouth, and is usually black or dark brown in color. Much of the body, limbs, and tail may be mottled with small, irregular flecks of tan, grayish-yellow or gray. But some specimens lack these flecks. The belly is usually black, but small flecks may be present.

Adult small-mouthed salamanders range in total length from 110-140 mm (4½-5½ inches). The record length for this species is 178 mm (7 inches; Conant, 1975).

Habits and Habitat.—The small-mouthed salamander lives under rotten logs and rocks, burrows in soil, or in piles of dead leaves. They are found in a wide variety of habitats including rocky hillsides, swamps, woodlands, grasslands, and even farmland. In Missouri they have been observed living in mole burrows (Bursewicz, *pers. comm.*).

As with the other mole salamanders, the food of this species consists of earthworms, slugs, and insects.

Breeding.—In Missouri the small-mouthed salamander breeds in early spring, usually from late February through March. Large numbers of these salamanders may congregate at suitable breeding sites which include temporary ponds and pools as well as ditches and streams. Several hundred eggs may be laid by one female and up to 700 eggs have been reported (Collins, 1974). The eggs are usually laid in small clumps in shallow water. They take several

weeks to hatch into gilled, pond-type larvae. The larvae take two to three months to transform into young adults and begin life on land.

Remarks.—Easterla (1970) reported finding an albino small-mouthed salamander in Stoddard County, Missouri.

Missouri Distribution.—This species is found throughout Missouri except for most of the Ozarkian Plateau and the extreme north-western corner of the state.

Fig. 19. Adult Eastern Tiger Salamander, *Ambystoma tigrinum tigrinum*.

EASTERN TIGER SALAMANDER
Ambystoma tigrinum tigrinum (Green)

Description.—A medium to large, dark salamander with yellow or olive blotches. Ground color is black or dark brown. The large spots or blotches vary greatly in size and shape, and are found over the head, body and tail. Blotch color ranges from bright yellow to dull olive-brown. The belly is dark gray or black with yellow mottling. Costal grooves number from 11-14. As with all members of the genus *Ambystoma*, males usually have longer tails than females, and during the breeding season the males have a swollen cloaca.

Adult specimens of this species range in size from 180-210 mm (7-8¼ inches). The record length is 330 mm (13 inches; Conant, 1975).

Habits and Habitat.—Eastern tiger salamanders are found in a wide variety of habitats including woodlands, swamps, farmlands, in the vicinity of farm ponds and may sometimes be found in wells, basements, and root cellars. These harmless salamanders spend most of their time in burrows under logs and rocks and are active only at night. Eastern tiger salamanders become migratory during autumn rains, moving to ponds where breeding will take place the following spring. Apparently, they remain in the vicinity of these ponds until spring.

Food of this species may be any animal small enough for them to swallow. Common foods include earthworms, insects, spiders, slugs, and snails.

Breeding.—Males can be observed migrating to breeding ponds in the fall. The breeding ponds usually lack fish. Breeding occurs between February and April. Up to 1,000 eggs may be laid by one female (Collins, 1974). The eggs are usually laid in small clusters on submerged branches or aquatic plants. The rate of development of the eggs averages two to four weeks, and is dependent on water temperature.

The pond-type larvae prey on a wide variety of aquatic animal life. In Missouri, metamorphosis into juveniles takes place in July

or August, although occasionally the larvae may not transform until the following summer. Neoteny, or the condition of sexually mature larvae, has been reported in eastern tiger salamanders, but to date this condition has not been found in Missouri.

Missouri Distribution.—The eastern tiger salamander is found throughout the state of Missouri.

FIG. 20. Central Newt, *Notophthalmus viridescens louisianensis.*

FAMILY SALAMANDRIDAE
NEWTS

In North America this family is represented by two genera: *Taricha* with species on the west coast, and *Notophthalmus* (Fig. 20) with species occurring from the east coast to the Great Plains.

Unlike most salamanders, which have smooth skin, the newts have rough, almost bumpy skin. Adults of the West Coast newts (*Taricha*) spend their lives on land in mosses and under logs, while adult *Notophthalmus* are usually aquatic.

The Central Newt, *Notophthalmus viridescens louisianensis,* is the only representative of this family in Missouri.

FIG. 21. Adult Central Newt, *Notophthalmus viridescens louisianensis*.

CENTRAL NEWT
Notophthalmus viridescens louisianensis (Wolterstorff)

Description.—The adult is a small, aquatic salamander without costal grooves or gills. It has an olive-brown back and a bright orange-yellow belly. There is a distinct separation between the dark color of the back and yellow of the belly where they meet along the sides of the body. A number of very small red spots ringed with black may or may not be present along the back on both sides of the spine. Usually the entire body is covered with numerous small black spots that may be somewhat larger on the belly than on the back. A dark brown or black line is present from the nostril through the eye to the fore limbs. The eyes are often orange-yellow in color.

During the breeding season, adult males can be distinguished by the presence of very high fins on the tail, large, swollen hind limbs, and cloacal lips; females appear heavy-bodied. The "eft" or middle stage of this salamander lives on land. Its dull brown color, more rounded tail, rough, rather dry skin, and lack of any secondary sexual characteristics distinguish it from the adults. Efts range in length from 35-86 mm (1⅜-3⅜ inches). Adults are normally between 70-100 mm (2⅝-4 inches; Conant, 1975) in length.

Habits and Habitat.—The food of adult newts consists of small aquatic invertebrates such as insects, small mollusks, crawfish, and various worms. The terrestrial efts feed on small insects and tiny snails found under logs and rocks. The aquatic larvae eat smaller aquatic invertebrates.

Adult central newts are found in farm or woodland ponds, swamps, and occasionally water-filled ditches. They are seldom numerous in ponds that harbor fish or that lack aquatic plants. The efts take shelter under logs, rocks, or piles of dead leaves in wooded areas around ponds inhabited by the adults. A small pond, if not disturbed, may hold a surprisingly high number of adult newts. They are active by day or night, and may be observed from shore as they swim near the surface, come up for air, or remain still in mid-water. They remain active throughout the year and have been observed in winter swimming about under the ice (Conant, 1975).

Breeding.—The courtship and life cycle of the central newt is more complex than that of most salamander species. Breeding takes place in the spring. A male will swim after a female, mount her back, clasp her body with his hind legs, and then will fan his tail toward the female. Tail fanning may help to propel a sexually stimulating odor secreted from the male's cloaca to the female; this induces the female to allow the courtship to continue toward completion. Eventually the female will begin fanning her tail, which induces the male to begin swimming about. At this time, the male's cloaca becomes more swollen, he leaves the female, and, moving forward, begins more rapid undulations. The female must follow him, and, if she touches his tail with her head, the male can then complete his courtship act by depositing a spermatophore. This sperm packet is then picked up by the female with her cloacal lips as she moves over the spot where it was deposited. After the eggs are internally fertilized, they are laid singly on aquatic plants and hatch between three to five weeks later. From 200-375 eggs may be laid by a single female during early summer (Bishop, 1943).

FIG. 22. Eft stage of the Central Newt.

The gilled, pond-type larvae remain in the water until the end of summer. They then metamorphose into the eft land stage. The efts remain on land from one to three years, then return to the water to take up an adult existence. Brandon and Bremer (1966) reported neotenic central newts from southern Illinois, but this has not been reported for Missouri populations.

Remarks.—Many swamps and ponds that were once habitat for central newts have been drained and cleared or stocked with game fish. These alterations are causing the eventual eradication of this species. In years to come it may be necessary to set aside areas in order to insure the survival of these interesting salamanders in Missouri.

Missouri Distribution.—The central newt is found throughout Missouri with the exception of the northwestern corner of the glaciated region.

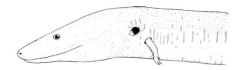

Fig. 23. Three-toed Amphiuma, *Amphiuma tridactylum.*

Family Amphiumidae
AMPHIUMAS

This strictly North American family is represented by only one genus, *Amphiuma,* which consists of three recognized species: the one-toed amphiuma, *Amphiuma pholeter;* the two-toed amphiuma, *A. means;* and the three-toed amphiuma, *A. tridactylum* (Fig. 23). Their combined range covers the southeastern and southern United States from North Carolina to east Texas. The three-toed amphiuma ranges into southeastern Missouri.

The amphiuma is the longest salamander in North America, and has been known to reach over 116 cm (45 inches; Conant, 1975). It has tiny, almost useless legs, small eyes (which lack eyelids), and smooth skin.

Fig. 24. Adult Three-toed Amphiuma, *Amphiuma tridactylum.*

THREE-TOED AMPHIUMA
Amphiuma tridactylum Cuvier

Description.—A completely aquatic, long cylindrical-shaped salamander with a somewhat pointed head, and very small front and
hind legs (with three toes on each limb). Color on the upper part
of an amphiuma is dull dark brown to black, while the belly is
lighter brown or gray. Adults have no gills (they have lungs), but
gill slits or openings on each side of the head are retained.

The three-toed amphiuma ranges in length from 46-76 cm (18-30
inches). The record length is 106 cm (41¾ inches; Conant, 1975).

Habits and Habitat.—Three-toed amphiumas spend the daylight
hours buried in silt or hiding under submerged roots, debris, or
aquatic plants. Their head and part of their neck may be exposed,
and periodically they must come to the surface for air. They venture forth at night in search of small fish, crawfish, tadpoles, snails,
aquatic insects, earthworms, and other aquatic animals.

This salamander makes its home in still waters, such as ditches,
sloughs, and swamps. In Missouri, cypress swamps are an especially
favorite haunt of the species.

These animals are difficult to collect in the wild because they
are alert, fast, slippery, and may bite viciously. Aquatic snakes are
known to prey on amphiumas.

Breeding.—Very little is known about the breeding habits of the
three-toed amphiuma in Missouri. In areas where it has been studied (western Tennessee) it is known to breed in late summer and

early fall. A female lays an average of 200 eggs (Salthe, 1974), usually under a rotten log near water. Once the eggs are covered by water they complete development and hatch. Larvae have gills and are between 63-75 mm (2½-3 inches) long.

Remarks.—The population size of these interesting salamanders in  Missouri is not clear. Probably due to the destruction of the native cypress swamps in the southeastern corner of the state, this species is on the decline. The cypress swamps that serve as the natural habitat of three-toed amphiumas and other wildlife should be preserved, and specific protection should be given to the three-toed amphiuma in this state.

Missouri Distribution.—The three-toed amphiuma prefers cypress swamps and ditches in the Mississippi River lowlands of Missouri.

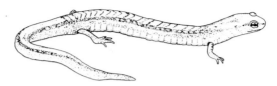

Fɪɢ. 25. Gray-bellied Salamander, *Eurycea multiplicata griseogaster*.

Fᴀᴍɪʟʏ Pʟᴇᴛʜᴏᴅᴏɴᴛɪᴅᴀᴇ
LUNGLESS SALAMANDERS

This successful family of salamanders is represented by 18 genera containing about 80 species. The family probably originated in the southern Appalachian Mountains of the eastern United States and has spread out over the entire eastern half of North America, the west coast, and into Mexico, Central America and northern South America. A few species also occur in southern Europe.

The adults lack lungs and most lack gills; the oxygen they require is taken from their environment through the skin and the mucous membrane of the mouth. Another character exclusive to this family is the presence of a groove in the skin running from each nostril down to the lip. In some species, associated with this groove (called the naso-labial groove) is a projection of skin which extends the groove below the upper lip. These projections are called *cirri* and are more pronounced on adult males. The groove and cirri may be associated with the sense of smell.

Lungless salamanders are found in a wide variety of moist habitats. Woodlands, springs, rock outcroppings with seepage, caves, and cold streams are habitats commonly associated with this group.

This family is represented in Missouri by 4 genera with 9 species.

FIG. 26. Adult Long-tailed Salamander, *Eurycea longicauda longicauda*.

LONG-TAILED SALAMANDER
Eurycea longicauda (Green)

Description.—A medium sized salamander with a long tail. Coloration is usually yellow, but may vary from greenish-yellow to orange-yellow. The belly is plain yellow. Dark brown or black markings and spots are found along the back and sides. Prominent vertical bars are present on the tail. Costal grooves number 13-14. Young of this species have fewer and smaller dark markings and a proportionately shorter tail.

Adult total length ranges from 102-160 mm (4-6¼ inches). The record length is 197 mm (7¾ inches; Conant, 1975).

Habits and Habitat.—The long-tailed salamander is nocturnal, but may emerge from hiding during the day after a heavy rain. It is usually found under rocks near streams, springs, and seepages in forested areas, and has been found in the twilight areas of caves. These salamanders are quite agile, and are able to escape predators by using their tails for quick jumps. If grasped by the tail, they will twist it off. Tailless specimens and those with partially regrown tails are often found. Food consists mainly of various small arthropods.

Breeding.—Breeding habits of this species in Missouri are unknown. In other states it breeds in the spring, laying its eggs singly or in small clusters on the undersurface of submerged rocks in clear streams or springs. The larvae are stream-type and may require up to two years to metamorphose into juveniles (Smith, 1961). Length at metamorphosis ranges from 65-75 mm (2½-3 inches).

FIG. 27. Adult Dark-sided Salamander, *Eurycea longicauda melanopleura.*

Subspecies.—The dark-sided salamander, *Eurycea longicauda melanopleura* (Cope) is wide-ranging in Missouri. This subspecies can be distinguished from the long-tailed salamander *(E. l. longicauda)* by the presence of larger and more numerous dark spots on the back, and by large amounts of dark pigment on the sides of the body from the head onto the tail. The sides are often spotted with white flecks. Vertical bars on the tail are more irregular in shape and may form dark vermiculations. Ground color may vary from a yellowish green to yellowish brown. The belly is a dull yellow with numerous dark flecks.

The dark-sided salamander is slightly smaller than the long-tailed salamander, with a length from 90-150 mm (3⅝-5⅞ inches); Conant, 1975). Intergradation between these subspecies is known from many areas of southeastern Missouri (see map).

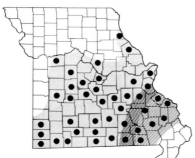

Missouri Distribution.—The long-tailed salamander is restricted to southeastern Missouri except for the Mississippi River lowlands. The dark-sided salamander is found throughout most of southern and eastern Missouri.

Fɪɢ. 28. Adult Cave Salamander, *Eurycea lucifuga.*

CAVE SALAMANDER
Eurycea lucifuga Rafinesque

Description.—This species is of medium size, has a long tail, and is normally bright orange. Cave salamanders vary in coloration from a yellow-orange to orange-red. Distinct dark brown or black spots irregularly cover most of the body. The belly is usually yellow-orange and without spots. Costal grooves number from 13-14. The end of the tail is often black.

Adult cave salamanders range in length from 100-150 mm (4-6 inches). The record is 181 mm (7⅛ inches; Conant, 1975).

Young cave salamanders are yellow in color and have shorter tails. Adult females are often larger than males, and males have a more prominent cirri. Males can also be distinguished from females by the presence of a swollen vent.

Habits and Habitat.—The range of this species is confined to areas of limestone outcroppings. Although usually found in caves, the cave salamander can also be found in wooded areas, along rocky streams and springs, in wells, and even swamps. Cave-dwelling individuals are usually encountered in the twilight zone, but have also been found far back in areas of permanent darkness. They are good climbers, able to cling to walls with their wet bodies, and capable of supporting themselves with their long tail to stalactites or stalagmites. When found away from caves, this species is nocturnal and spends daylight hours under rocks or rotten logs. It may be seen during the day after a heavy rain on rocks or boulders. If pursued, these salamanders will jump and scamper away with remarkable agility.

The food of this species consists of a variety of small arthropods.

Breeding.—Reproduction in this species has not been studied to any extent in Missouri, but breeding generally takes place in the autumn. A female lays from 50-90 eggs, either in cave streams, springs, or rocky streams outside of caves. The eggs are laid singly under rocks or on the stream bottom. The larvae are gilled and live from one to two years in the water. When ready to leave the water, the young may be from 2-2½ inches long (Barbour, 1971; Collins, 1974).

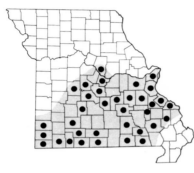

Remarks.—As with all animals living in caves, the cave salamander should never be molested in any manner. The ecological balance in a cave is extremely fragile, and any disturbance could be dangerous to this balance.

Missouri Distribution.—The cave salamander is found throughout most of the southern half of Missouri, with the exception of the Mississippi River lowlands. It is a common amphibian of the Ozark Plateau.

Fig. 29. Adult Gray-bellied Salamander, *Eurycea multiplicata griseogaster.*

GRAY-BELLIED SALAMANDER
Eurycea multiplicata griseogaster Moore and Hughes

Description.—A small, dark, slender salamander, generally yellowish-tan to dark brown or gray in color. The dorsal stripe may be yellow-tan to brown, and is bordered by dark brown lines. Along the dorsum may be a medial row of dark brown chevrons which correspond to the costal grooves. Costal grooves number 19-20. Small white flecks are present along the sides and tail. The belly is gray, but may have some yellow coloration.

Adults range in total length from 48-83 mm (1⅞-3¼ inches). The record length is 97 mm (3 13/16 inches; Conant, 1975). Neotenic individuals may reach a larger size than metamorphosed individuals (Dundee, 1965).

Habits and Habitat.—The gray-bellied salamander hides under rocks and logs in or near cold, clear streams or cave springs. In Missouri it is most often encountered in the twilight zone and streams of caves. When outside caves, these salamanders are nocturnal and may venture away from streams on rainy nights. Neoteny is common in this species, and Dundee (1965) reports that entire cave populations may be neotenic. Small arthropods are eaten by both adults and larvae.

Breeding.—Little is known about the reproduction of this species in Missouri. In general, fertilization is internal and the eggs are laid along the undersurface of rocks in cave streams and springs. The larvae are the gilled stream-type. Larvae either metamorphose into adults or retain the gills and mature as neotenic individuals. Ireland (1976) studied this species in Arkansas, and found that breeding may last from September to April. Females lay from 3-21 eggs in strands. In populations studied in Arkansas, larvae metamorphosed in five to eight months.

Missouri Distribution.—The gray-bellied salamander occurs in the central and southwestern portion of the Ozark Plateau.

FIG. 30. Adult Oklahoma Salamander, *Eurycea tynerensis*.

OKLAHOMA SALAMANDER
Eurycea tynerensis Moore and Hughes

Description.—A small, slender, gilled, and permanently aquatic salamander. The back and sides are usually gray. This is due to extensive stippling covering the cream or light tan ground color. The amount of stippling may vary between individuals. The belly is pale and without markings. One or two lines of small white spots run along the sides. Costal grooves number 19-21. Poorly developed dorsal and ventral fins are present on the tail. A broad, dark stripe is usually found on each side of the tail.

This neotenic salamander reaches a total length of 44-79 mm (1¾-3⅛ inches; Conant, 1975).

Habits and Habitat.—The Oklahoma salamander makes its home in cold, clear streams and springs, hiding under rocks, in loose stones, or around aquatic plants. Various small aquatic arthropods are utilized as food.

Breeding.—Little is known about the reproduction of this salamander. Dundee (1965) reports that the eggs are attached to stones in the water. The larvae are said to resemble the adults in both shape and color (Bishop, 1943).

Remarks.—This neotenic salamander has been artifically induced to metamorphose and acquire adult characteristics (Kezer, 1952). Due to its restricted distribution in Missouri, this species may require protection.

Missouri Distribution.—This species is known from McDonald and Berry counties, and is presumed to occur in adjacent Newton and Stone counties.

Fig. 31. Adult Four-toed Salamander, *Hemidactylium scutatum*. Photographed on mirror to show belly.

Four-Toed Salamander
Hemidactylium scutatum (Schlegel)

Description.—A small, delicate salamander with a thick, round tail. Four toes on both front and hind feet. The snout appears short and blunt. General coloration is yellowish-tan to brown on the back with many faint, irregular black spots. Sides of body are grayish-brown with black strippling and the belly is pure white with numerous large, irregular black spots. The tail is distinctly constricted near its base. Costal grooves number 12-14. Males of this species are smaller, more slender, and have longer tails than females (Bishop, 1943).

Adult four-toed salamanders range in length from 51-89 mm (2-3¼ inches). The record length is 102 mm (4 inches; Conant, 1975).

Habits and Habitat.—This salamander is commonly associated with sphagnum (peat) bogs. However, in Missouri the four-toed salamander has been located in mosses along spring fed streams, as well as in woodland bogs. It may also be found hiding under rotten logs, rocks, and in leaf litter in hardwood forests, but is seldom found far from a bog, stream, or seepage area. The four-toed salamander preys on small arthropods and molluscs.

Breeding.—The four-toed salamander mates in the autumn. As with all lungless salamanders, fertilization is internal. Females move to a stream or bog in the spring, soon after emerging from hibernation. About 30 eggs are laid in a protected pocket of moss very close to water. Eggs are usually attached to a strand or root of moss (Bishop, 1943). The female remains with the eggs until they hatch, usually in about four weeks. Upon hatching, the gilled larvae find their way to, or drop into the water, where they remain for a period of up to two months. The larvae can be distinguished by the presence of a high fin or keel which begins on the back and extends down the entire length of the tail. After metamorphosing, the juveniles become terrestrial but may take over two years to reach sexual maturity (Bishop, 1943).

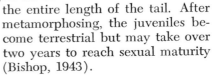

Remarks.—This species is considered threatened by the Missouri Department of Conservation principally because of the small number of populations.

Missouri Distribution.—This species has been found in only a few counties in the portion of the Ozark Plateau.

Fig. 32. Adult Ozark Red-backed Salamander, *Plethodon dorsalis angusticlavius.*

OZARK RED-BACKED SALAMANDER
Plethodon dorsalis angusticlavius Grobman

Description.—A small, dark, slender, woodland salamander with a narrow, somewhat lobed middorsal stripe. The dorsal stripe usually has irregular or wavy edges, especially closer to the head. Coloration of the dorsal stripe may range from yellow, to yellow-orange, to orange, to red. Dark brown or black pigment may invade the dorsal stripe causing it to look lobed, or may cover a large part of the stripe. Normally the width of the dorsal stripe is 30% or less than the width of the body and is widest near the hind legs. Some specimens may lack a dorsal stripe. The belly has white and black mottling. The sides of the body are generally dark gray or brownish gray, with some orange or red, and small white flecks. Costal grooves number 17-19. The sexes are difficult to distinguish, but males are smaller and more slender than females. The Ozark red-backed salamander ranges in size from 60-98 mm (2⅜-3⅞ inches; Conant, 1975).

Habits and Habitat.—Conant (1975) stated that the Ozark red-backed salamander is found "usually in or near caves of the Central Highlands." Myers (1958) also found this species in Missouri caves. I have found this salamander living in or under rotten logs, under rocks and leaf litter in seepages near small streams, as well as on steep hillsides. The Ozark red-backed salamander may have a preference for living in cooler and damper habitats than the southern red-backed salamander *(P. serratus).* Food consists of very small arthropods.

Breeding.—Nothing is known about the reproduction of this salamander in Missouri. Breeding presumably takes place in the fall, fertilization is internal, and the eggs are laid during the spring in rotten logs.

Remarks.—Research is currently being carried out to gain a better understanding about the relationship of this subspecies with the zigzag salamander *(P. d. dorsalis)* from the east central United States (Highton, *pers. comm.*). See *Remarks* under the southern red-backed salamander account.

Missouri Distribution.—The Ozark red-backed salamander is found in the south central and southwestern portion of the Ozark Plateau.

FIG. 33. Adult Slimy Salamander, *Plethodon glutinosus glutinosus*.

SLIMY SALAMANDER
Plethodon glutinosus glutinosus (Green)

Description.—A black, medium sized woodland salamander with a long rounded tail and numerous silvery-colored flecks irregularly distributed over the head, back, limbs, and tail. The chin and belly are dark gray in color. Costal grooves usually number sixteen. Males can be distinguished from females by the presence of a light colored swelling (mental gland) under the chin of the males during the breeding season.

Adult slimy salamanders range in length from 122-172 mm (4¾-6¾ inches). The record length is 206 mm (8¼ inches; Conant, 1975). This is the largest plethodontid salamander found in Missouri.

Habits and Habitat.—The slimy salamander is commonly found under rocks or logs in damp ravines and moist wooded hillsides. During dry weather in summer they may retreat underground or burrow into large piles of leaf litter to find a damp place to live. They venture out of hiding at night or after heavy rains. This species has been found in the twilight zones of Missouri caves (Myers, 1958).

Skin glands of the slimy salamander secrete a thick, very sticky substance that adheres to human skin like glue and is difficult to remove. This species eats small arthropods and worms.

Breeding.—The slimy salamander lays its eggs under rotten logs or other damp places. The young do not go through an aquatic larval stage. Little is known about the breeding habits of this species in

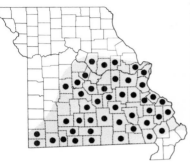

Missouri. They are known to lay their eggs (from 10-20) in early summer. The female attends the eggs during the incubation period. Hatching probably takes place in late summer or early autumn. The young look very much like the adults but have shorter tails (Barbour, 1971).

Missouri Distribution.—The slimy salamander is found throughout the Ozark Plateau of Missouri but is generally absent in the Mississippi River lowlands.

Fig. 34. Adult Southern Red-backed Salamander, *Plethodon serratus.*

SOUTHERN RED-BACKED SALAMANDER
Plethodon serratus Grobman

Description.—A small, dark, slender salamander with a long, rounded tail. A distinct, somewhat narrow, red middorsal stripe with saw-toothed edges that correspond with the costal grooves is usually present. The middorsal stripe, when present, is usually red or orange-red. The sides are brownish-gray, with some reddish pigment. The belly is covered with gray mottling. Costal grooves number 18-19. The sexes are difficult to distinguish; males are normally smaller and more slender than females.

Adults range in length from 70-102 mm (2¾-4 inches; Conant, 1975).

Habits and Habitat.—This terrestrial salamander is commonly found in forests where it hides under rocks, clumps of mosses, and rotten logs. During the drier parts of the summer it may be found near seepages, springs, or in damp soil. Myers (1958) found this species in the twilight zone of Missouri caves, but this is not a common occurrence. A variety of small arthropods are eaten by this species.

Breeding.—Courtship and breeding take place in late autumn, and females retain the sperm internally until the following year. Fertilization of the eggs takes place as they are laid during the next summer (June and July). The female selects a small cavity in a rotten log, a patch of moss, or under rock and deposits 8-14 eggs in a clump on the roof of the cavity. The female remains with the eggs until they hatch. Since the eggs are laid on land, the very short larval period takes place in the egg. The young red-backed salamanders usually hatch in August and resemble the adults except for a somewhat shorter tail and a more brightly colored middorsal stripe. It takes up to two years for the young to reach sexual maturity.

Remarks.—The red-backed salamander of south-central and southeastern Missouri has been identified as *Plethodon cinereus cinereus* by most authors (Highton, 1962; Smith, 1963; Johnson and Bader 1974; Conant, 1975). Recent investigations by Highton and Webster (1976) have shown that the Missouri population is more closely associated with the Arkansas population *(P. c. serratus)*, as well as other southern isolated populations. *P. c. serratus* has recently been elevated to a species level, encompassing several southern isolated populations previously identified as a subspecies of *P. cinereus* (Highton and Webster, 1976). The common name for this species, the southern red-backed salamander, was proposed by Highton *(pers. comm.)*.

The two species of red-backed salamander found in Missouri may be easily confused. In the southern red-backed salamander the dorsal stripe is usually uniform in width and has serrated edges. The dorsal stripe of the Ozark red-backed salamander is usually

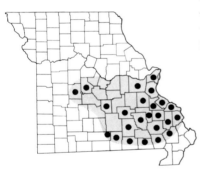

very thin (less than 30% of the width of the body), may be broken up into lobes, and is always widest near the hind legs. These two species may be found together in several Missouri counties, but the possibility of hybridization between the two forms is remote (Highton, *pers. comm.*).

Missouri Distribution.—The southern red-backed salamander is found in the south central and southeastern section of the state, with the exception of the Mississippi River lowlands.

FIG. 35. Adult Grotto Salamander, *Typhlotriton spelaeus.*

GROTTO SALAMANDER
Typhlotriton spelaeus Stejneger

Description.—Adults of this species are tannish-white to pink in color, and are blind or nearly so. These *troglodytic* salamanders lack gills as adults. The head is rather wide and flat, the eyes are small, and the tail is long, rounded and finless. Costal grooves number from 16-19.

Males can be told from females by the presence of fleshy projections on the upper lip *(cirri)*, and a larger, swollen, vent (cloaca). Adults of both sexes have reduced eyes, which are covered or partially covered, by a fusion of the eye lids. The eyes may appear sunken into the head.

The larvae of this species have gills, functional eyes, and broad tail fins. Their legs are thin and weak. Larvae have more pigment than adults and color varies from brown to dark gray. Dark pigmentation may form spots or streaking along the sides and tail.

Adult grotto salamanders range in total length from 80-120 mm (3-4¾ inches). The record length is 135 mm (5 5/16 inches; Conant, 1975).

Habits and Habitat.—This is the only species of blind salamander living in Missouri. Adults of the grotto salamander are true troglodytes; found only in wet caves where they live in total darkness. This species requires caves which have a spring or stream running through them and are found in greater abundance in caves that have a large number of bats. The food of adults is made up of various small insects found in caves (Smith, 1948; Brandon, 1971).

Breeding.—Little is known about the reproduction of this species in Missouri. Brandon (1971) correlates the breeding of the grotto salamander with the period of greatest food supply (late spring and early summer). To date, the eggs have not been observed. Fertilization is internal, and the eggs are probably attached to stones in or near water in caves. The larvae are stream-type and normally inhabit cave streams, though they are occasionally found in springs or streams that flow out of caves.

Brandon (1970) found that the larvae may take from two to three years to transform into adults. During this time they range from 36-56 mm snout-vent length (Brandon, 1966). Larvae probably eat tiny fresh water shrimp *(Gammaris)* and other small aquatic invertebrates.

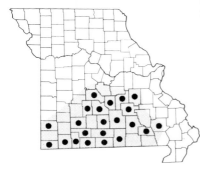

Remarks.—Because of the delicate balance of cave ecosystems, the grotto salamander should be protected from any form of molestation, including any alteration of caves or their water supplies. The type locality for this species is Berry County, Missouri.

Missouri Distribution.—This species is found in wet caves of the Ozark Plateau.

FIG. 36. Mudpuppy, *Necturus maculosus maculosus.*

FAMILY PROTEIDAE
MUDPUPPY, WATERDOG

This family contains only two genera. The first, *Proteus*, contains but one species called the European olm, a slender, pale white, blind cave salamander. This species lives in cave streams, has bright red gills, and three toes on each of its four limbs.

The other genus of this family is *Necturus*, which consists of four species, all exclusively North American (Fig. 36). They are commonly known as mudpuppies or waterdogs and are found throughout most of the eastern United States. They have gills, are permanently aquatic, and may be found in a variety of habitats, including streams, rivers, ponds, and lakes. In the northern part of its range the mudpuppy has been netted at a depth of several hundred feet in some larger lakes.

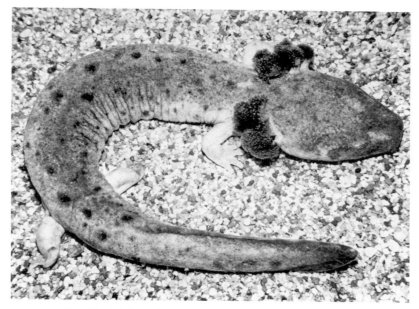

Fig. 37. Adult Mudpuppy, *Necturus maculosus maculosus*.

MUDPUPPY
Necturus maculosus (Rafinesque)

Description.—A completely aquatic species, the mudpuppy is gray-brown above and pale gray below. Most of the body has numerous small, irregular dark brown to black spots which sometimes appear on the belly. Behind the head are plumes of red gills. These gills vary in size, depending on the oxygen content of the salamander's aquatic habitat. There are four toes on both the front and hind limbs. The eyes are small and lack eye-lids. All *Necturus* are *paedogenetic* (permanently larval).

Adult mudpuppies range in size from 200-300 mm (8-13 inches; Conant, 1975). The record length in Missouri is 420 mm (16½ inches; Johnson, 1975a).

Habits and Habitat.—In Missouri these salamanders are normally found in large streams, rivers, or reservoirs. They are inactive during the day, usually remaining hidden under submerged logs, rocks, and tree roots in deep pools. They become active at night when they feed. Mudpuppies are known to remain active throughout the year, but it is not known if they feed during the winter in Missouri. Food of the mudpuppy consists of any aquatic animal small enough to be captured and swallowed, including aquatic insects and their larvae, crawfish, molluscs, small fish, and worms.

Breeding.—Little is known about the breeding habits of the mudpuppy in Missouri, but the species has been studied elsewhere. Mating takes place in the fall, and fertilization is internal, but the eggs are not laid until the following spring. The 75-100 eggs laid are usually attached to the underside of a submerged rock. The female remains with the eggs until hatching, which may take one and a half to two months (Smith, 1961).

Subspecies.—There are two subspecies of *Necturus maculosus* found in Missouri, the mudpuppy, *N. m. maculosus*, described above, and the Red River waterdog, *Necturus maculosus louisianensis* Viosca. The waterdog may be distinguished from the mudpuppy by a lighter grey-brown or red-brown ground color. Dark spots on the upper parts of the body are more distinct and more numerous. The belly has a wide, light, unspotted area down the center which may be light gray to gray with edges of pale pink. The Red River waterdog is somewhat smaller than the mudpuppy, with a maximum length of about 280 mm (11 inches; Conant, 1975).

Remarks.—The mudpuppy and Red River waterdog are harmless to humans. Fishermen often catch them on baited hook-and-line or in minnow traps. They do not harm natural fish populations and are

an integral part of the aquatic fauna of Missouri.

Missouri Distribution.—The mudpuppy is found throughout most of Missouri except the northwestern corner of the state. It is replaced by the Red River waterdog in the extreme southern part of the state (hatch lines). Intergradation between the two subspecies has not yet been reported in Missouri, but an assumed area of integradation is shown by the overlap of shading.

Fig. 38. Eastern Spadefoot Toad, *Scaphiopus holbrookii holbrookii.*

Family Pelobatidae
SPADEFOOT TOADS

Members of this family have been divided into two subfamilies: the Megophryinae of Asia; and the Pelobatinae, with representatives in Europe, North Africa, and North America.

Spadefoot toads are not true toads (Family Bufonidae), but resemble them in general appearance and are equally able to bury themselves *(fossorial)* in loose dirt. The name spadefoot is derived from a special tubercle found on the hind feet, which is spade-shaped and used to dig into soil. Spadefoot toads have smoother skin than true toads, and the pupils of their eyes are vertical.

In North America this family is represented by only one genus, *Scaphiopus,* with 5 species, two of which occur in Missouri.

FIG. 39. Adult Plains Spadefoot Toad, *Scaphiopus bombifrons*.

PLAINS SPADEFOOT TOAD
Scaphiopus bombifrons Cope

Description.—The plains spadefoot toad can be distinguished from the eastern spadefoot toad by the presence of a raised area (boss) between the eyes, and by the wedge-shaped spade at the base of each hind foot. The general coloration of the plains spadefoot toad ranges from gray to tannish-gray to brown, although some green may be mixed into the background color. A number of irregular dark brown markings are usually present on the back and hind legs. Two or four faint light stripes may be found on the back. The belly is white. Small, round warts, often reddish in color, are usually found on the back and sides. Males can be distinguished from females by their swollen fore-feet and dark throats.

Adults range from 38-51 mm (1½-2 inches) in snout-vent length. The record size is 57 mm (2¼ inches; Conant, 1975).

Habits and Habitat.—This species is at home on the Great Plains, where it can be found in prairie or open flood plain situations. By day it remains hidden in burrows in sandy soil. It emerges at night, especially after heavy rains. A variety of insects make up its diet.

Breeding.—The plains spadefoot toad is stimulated to breed only after heavy, warm rains. The males congregate at temporary pools in flooded fields. If a female approaches a calling mate, he will clasp her just forward of her hind legs and they will enter the water. The female can produce up to 2,000 eggs which are fertilized by the male as they are laid. The eggs are usually attached to submerged vegetation in clumps of 10-250 (Collins, 1974). If conditions are favorable, the eggs hatch in one or two days. The rate of hatching and transformation is regulated by water temperature, amount of dissolved oxygen, and food supply. Tadpoles of spadefoot toads are carnivorous. If the temporary pool in which they hatch evaporates too fast, the tadpoles become overcrowded and cannibalism may result.

The voice of the breeding plains spadefoot toad can be described as a long rasping or nasal *"garvank,"* called at intervals from one-half to one second.

Missouri Distribution.—The plains spadefoot toad has been collected in northwestern Missouri and in a number of counties along the Missouri River.

Fig. 40. Adult Eastern Spadefoot Toad, *Scaphiopus holbrooki holbrookii.*

EASTERN SPADEFOOT TOAD
Scaphiopus holbrookii holbrookii (Harlan)

Description.—A stout, toad-like amphibian with large protruding eyes, vertically elliptical pupils, short legs, and large feet. Small inconspicuous, parotoid glands are present. There is no boss between the eyes. The general ground color is light brown to yellow-brown. Head, back, and upper parts of legs are mottled with dark brown. The amount of dark brown on the dorsum may be great enough to form two to three light yellow-brown longitudinal stripes. Belly pale white to gray. The inner surface of each hind foot has a sickle-shaped spur or spade.

Males can be distinguished during the breeding season by their swollen fore-feet and by the presence of a dark, horny covering on the inner surface of each hand.

Adult eastern spadefoot toads range from 44-57 mm (1¾-2¼ inches) in snout-vent length. The record size is 73 mm (2⅞ inches; Conant, 1975).

Habits and Habitat.—Eastern spadefoot toads spend most of their time in burrows dug with their specialized hind feet. They are nocturnal, and become active on warm, damp, or rainy nights. They are occasionally found in wooded areas, but seem to prefer open fields where loose sand and soil facilitates burrowing. Food includes a variety of insects.

Breeding.—Breeding takes place after heavy rains, usually between May and August in southeastern Missouri if rains are sufficient to stimulate breeding aggregations.

The eastern spadefoot toad breeds in temporarily flooded fields or ditches. The eggs are fertilized by the male during amplexus as the female lays them. Eggs are layed in short strands which are attached to submerged vegetation. Hatching may take place in only a few days and the tadpoles may transform in less than three weeks (Smith, 1961).

The voice of the male eastern spadefoot toad can be described

as a quick series of coarse "*wank, wank, wank*" sounds. Wright and Wright (1942), described their call as sounding like a "young crow."

Remarks.—The eastern spadefoot toad has a restricted range in Missouri and, due to its low population size in this state, should be protected by the Missouri Department of Conservation.

Missouri Distribution.—This species has been collected in the southeastern corner of Missouri.

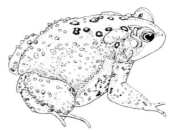

Fig. 41. American Toad, *Bufo americanus americanus.*

Family Bufonidae
TRUE TOADS

Members of this family are nearly world-wide in distribution, being absent only from New Zealand, Australia, Madagascar, and the polar regions. There are at least 15 species of these toads in the United States; all are members of the genus *Bufo.* In Missouri there are 3 species and 2 subspecies of toads.

Toads have dry skin compared to frogs, lack extensive webbing on the hind feet, have large glands on their shoulders (parotoid glands), numerous warts over most of their body, and toxic skin secretions that are irritating to mucous membrane. All species of toads found in Missouri are mainly nocturnal, seeking shelter during the day under piles of dead leaves, rocks and logs, or in loose soil. These amphibians are well known for their consumption of large numbers of insects. Contrary to popular belief, toads do not cause warts in humans.

Fig. 42. Adult Dwarf American Toad, *Bufo americanus charlesmithi*.

AMERICAN TOAD
Bufo americanus Holbrook

Description.—A medium sized toad with kidney-shaped parotoid glands behind the eyes. The bony cranial ridges between the eyes usually do not touch the parotoid glands but may be connected by a small spur. Large black or dark brown spots on the back usually encircle from one to three warts. A narrow, light stripe down the back may be present. The general color may be gray, light brown, brown, or reddish-brown. The belly is white with dark gray mottling. Adult males can be distinguished from adult females during the breeding season by an enlarged, horny pad on the inside of each hand, and the presence of a dark gray throat. Females are generally larger than males.

Adult American toads range in size from 51-89 mm (2-3½ inches). The record size is 111 mm (4⅜ inches; Conant, 1975).

Habits and Habitat.—The American toad prefers rocky wooded areas and is often found along the edge of hardwood forests. They hide during the day under rocks where there is loose, moist dirt or may burrow into a depression where dead leaves have accumulated. Like most toads, the American toad becomes active at dusk and into the night feeding on earthworms and insects.

Breeding.—In Missouri, male American toads begin calling during mid to late March. Breeding sites are usually small temporary ponds, slow, shallow streams, or ditches. The male grasps the female behind her front legs, and while they float on the water, the female begins laying eggs in long, double strands. As the eggs emerge from the female, they are fertilized by the male. From 2,000 to over 20,000 eggs may be laid by one female. The eggs hatch in about one week into tiny black tadpoles. The tadpoles remain in the water until early to mid-June, at which time they metamorphose into small toadlets. In Missouri, the peak breeding period is mid-April.

The call of the male American toad is described as a sustained, high-pitched musical trill (Smith, 1961).

Fig. 43. Dwarf American Toad male "calling".

Subspecies.—There are two subspecies of *Bufo americanus* in Missouri: the American toad, *Bufo americanus americanus* Holbrook as described above and the dwarf American toad, *Bufo americanus charlesmithi* Bragg.

The dwarf American toad is a smaller race of the American toad. The ground color is rich reddish-brown and the size and number of dark spots on the back are reduced or absent. The belly is cream colored with a small number of dark gray spots on the breast. The call of a male *B. a. charlesmithi* is similar to, but higher in pitch than, the American toad.

After examining a number of specimens of both races of American toads from many parts of Missouri, it is apparent that there is a wide band of intergradation between these two subspecies along a line from St. Louis to below Kansas City (see distribution map).

Remarks.—The two subspecies of the American toad in Missouri have been known to hybridize with the Fowler's toad *(Bufo woodhousei fowleri)* in many parts of the state. The offspring of this crossbreeding are very difficult to identify because they often have a number of characters of both species. Generally, hybridization

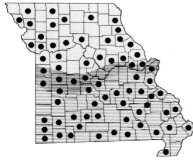

occurs when there is an overlap of breeding activity or where extensive habitat disturbance by man has occurred.

Missouri Distribution.—State wide. Generally, the American toad (stippling) may be found in counties north of the Missouri River, while the dwarf American toad (hatch lines) occurs in counties south of the Missouri River.

FIG. 44. Adult Great Plains Toad, *Bufo cognatus.*

GREAT PLAINS TOAD
Bufo cognatus Say

Description.—A medium sized toad with large dark blotches on the back and sides of the body. Each blotch is usually encircled with white or light tan and contains many warts. Blotch color may vary from gray, brown, dark green, green or yellowish. A light, narrow stripe may run down the back of some individuals. The parotoid glands are kidney-shaped and are connected to the bony cranial crest. The bony crests unite between the eyes and form a raised boss on the snout. The belly is cream colored with little or no gray spotting. Adult male *Bufo cognatus* are smaller than adult females. A dark throat and the presence of horny pads on the inside of each hand distinguishes males from females during the breeding season.

Adults range in length from 48-89 mm (1⅞-3½ inches). The record size is 114 mm (4½ inches; Conant, 1975).

Habits and Habitat.—Because of the limited range of this species in Missouri, little is known about its natural history in the state. In other states it has been reported to occur in mixed-grass and short-grass prairies. This species may frequent open flood plains (Collins, 1974). Wooded areas are usually avoided. As with most species of toads, the Great Plains toad hides in underground burrows by day but emerges at night to hunt for insects.

Breeding.—Rain filled ditches and pools are selected as breeding sites. Males begin their chorus in late April. Breeding aggregations may form as late as June (Collins, 1974). Breeding takes place after a female has been mounted by the male (amplexus) in the water. The eggs are laid in long strands in the water and are fertilized by the male as they are laid. A single female may lay up to 20,000 eggs. The eggs hatch in about a week and the tadpoles usually metamorphose to toadlets by early July.

The call of the Great Plains toad can be described as a loud, piercing, metallic, trill lasting from 20-50 seconds (Conant, 1975). The inflated vocal sac is sausage-shaped, and extends forward and above the snout.

Remarks.—In recent years this species has been reported in several counties along the Missouri River east of the Kansas City area. Metter, *et al.* (1970) reported that they have extended their range eastward, due to spring flooding of the Missouri River valley, and are now established in central Missouri.

Missouri Distribution.—The range of the Great Plains toad in Missouri consists of the extreme northwestern and western counties, and in central Missouri along the Missouri River valley.

FIG. 45. Adult Woodhouse's Toad, *Bufo woodhousei woodhousei.*

WOODHOUSE'S TOAD
Bufo woodhousei Girard

Description.—This medium sized toad has a number of irregular
dark brown or black spots on the back, containing from one to six
warts inside each spot. The general color varies from gray, tannish-
gray, or greenish-gray to brown. The belly is white, and usually
unspotted, although a single "breast" spot may be present on some
individuals. A tan or white stripe is usually present down the back.
The parotoid gland is oblong in shape and is connected to a rather
shallow bony cranial crest. Adult males are smaller than adult females, and males can be distinguished during the breeding season
by their dark throats and dark, horny pads on the inside of each
hand.

Adult Woodhouse's toads range in length from 60-100 mm (2½-4
inches). The record is 127 mm (5 inches; Conant, 1975).

Habits and Habitat.—This species seems to prefer sandy lowlands,
particularly river bottoms. It may also be encountered in open, dry
areas adjacent to marshes. As with other toads, it remains hidden in
burrows by day, becoming active at night to hunt for insect prey.

Breeding.—Although it may become active in late March, this species will not begin to breed until late April or early May, showing a peak of breeding activity in mid-May. In general, the Woodhouse's toad breeds later and at warmer temperatures than the American toad. Small groups of males congregate along the shore of shallow bodies of water (river sloughs, shallow ditches, ponds, and flooded fields). They produce their distinct call until a female is attracted. Amplexus is followed by egg laying. The eggs are laid in long strands and are fertilized by the male as they are laid. Up to 25,000 eggs may be laid by a female (Collins, 1974). The eggs hatch in about a week, and the black tadpoles begin to metamorphose into toadlets by late June or mid-July.

The call of the male Woodhouse's toad is a short, nasal *w-a-a-a-h*, lasting from one to two and one-half seconds (Conant, 1975).

FIG. 46. Adult Fowler's Toad, *Bufo woodhousei fowleri.*

Subspecies.—Two subspecies of *Bufo woodhousei* occur in Missouri: the nominate race, the Woodhouse's toad, *Bufo woodhousei woodhousei* Girard (described above); and the Fowler's toad, *Bufo woodhousei fowleri* Hinckley. Fowler's toad is very similar to Woodhouse's toad, especially in its habits, habitat requirements, and breeding. However, it can be distinguished from *Bufo w. woodhousei* by the presence of dark spots on the back which are usually larger and more uniform in shape and arranged in pairs down the back. Each spot contains 3 or more warts. General coloration is gray, greenish gray, or tannish gray. The light line down the back is white. The bony cranial crest of Fowler's toad seems to be slightly more developed than in Woodhouse's toad, but not as well developed as in the American toad. The belly is white and a "breast" spot is often present. The voice of a male Fowler's toad is very similar to Woodhouse's toad, but has a slightly higher pitch (Conant, 1975).

Remarks.—Both subspecies of *Bufo woodhousei* have been known to hybridize with the American toad (see species account for American toad).

Missouri Distribution.—Fowler's toad is the more widespread subspecies in the state, ranging over all of eastern and southern Missouri. Woodhouse's toad is restricted to the west central and northwestern part of the state. Conant (1975) did not show an area of intergradation between the two subspecies in Missouri, and only a few specimens were available from counties where intergradation may occur. Thus, the area of intergradation shown on the map is based on the few specimens examined by me and is included to stimulate others to study the relationship of these toads in Missouri.

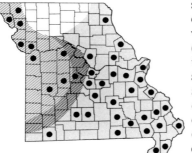

Fɪɢ. 47. Eastern Gray Treefrog, *Hyla versicolor versicolor*.

Fᴀᴍɪʟʏ Hʏʟɪᴅᴀᴇ
TREEFROGS, CHORUS FROGS, AND CRICKET FROGS

This family contains over 450 species, most of which are small in size. They are found on all continents where suitable habitats are present, but are most numerous in Central America and northern South America. The family seems to have originated in the tropics and has spread toward the poles.

Of the 6 genera of treefrogs and their allies found in North America, 3 are native to Missouri: *Hyla* (treefrogs), *Pseudacris* (chorus frogs), and *Acris* (cricket frogs). These three genera contain a total of eight species or subspecies found in Missouri.

Several of Missouri's treefrogs have the ability to change color, which seems to be associated with temperature, humidity, light, and even the temperament of the frog. The majority of species have adhesive pads on their fingers and toes, which are helpful in climbing about on plants. Their relatively long hind legs are also useful for climbing. In this family, females are larger than males. All types of small arthropods are eaten by these frogs.

Fig. 48. Adult Blanchard's Cricket Frog, *Acris crepitans blanchardi.*

BLANCHARD'S CRICKET FROG
Acris crepitans blanchardi (Harper)

Description.—A small, non-climbing, warty frog with a variety of colorations. Three important color patterns are always present: (1) a series of light and dark bars on the upper jaw, (2) a dark triangle between the eyes, and (3) a black or brown irregular stripe along the inside of the thigh. The general coloration may vary from gray to tan, greenish-tan, brown, to almost black. An irregular stripe usually present down the back may be green, yellow, orange, or red. The belly is white. The feet are strongly webbed, but the adhesive pads are small and poorly developed on the fingers and toes. During the breeding season the chins of the males may be spotted with gray and the throat may be yellowish in color.

Adult Blanchard's cricket frogs range in length from 16-38 mm (⅝-1½ inches; Conant, 1975).

Habits and Habitat.—This frog is usually active from late March to early November. During the spring and autumn, Blanchard's cricket frogs are active only during the day, but in warmer weather they are active both day and night. These alert little frogs will avoid their enemies by a series of quick, erratic hops. They prefer the open, sandy, or muddy edges of streams and ponds. The bulk of their food consists of a variety of small terrestrial insects (Johnson and Christiansen, 1976).

Breeding.—Even though Blanchard's cricket frogs can remain active during cool temperatures, they wait until the warm days of late spring to begin breeding. Males begin calling by mid-to-late April and the breeding period may last until late June. Males clasp females in amplexus, and egg laying and fertilization take place in the water. A female may lay up to 400 eggs, either singly or in small packets of up to six eggs on the surface of a pond or ditch. The eggs hatch in a few days, and the small tadpoles begin metamorphosis 5 to 10 weeks later.

The call of the male Blanchard's cricket frog is a metallic "*gick,*

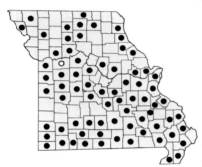

gick, gick," somewhat like the sound of small pebbles being struck rapidly together. Although their breeding period may last until mid-July, the males can be heard calling day and night throughout the summer.

Missouri Distribution.—Blanchard's cricket frog is presumably state wide in occurrence and common in most parts of Missouri.

Fig. 49. Adult Green Treefrog, *Hyla cinerea*.

GREEN TREEFROG
Hyla cinerea (Schneider)

Description.—A large member of the family, usually light to dark green in color. A white or pale yellow stripe running from the upper lip and down the side is always present. In most of the green treefrogs in Missouri, this stripe stops half way down the side, seldom reaching the groin. It may be outlined with a thin black line in some individuals. Another white or pale yellow stripe is present on the inside of the hind legs. The smooth back may have a few small gold spots. The belly is white or yellowish. Males calling at night may be light green to yellow in color. Distinct round adhesive pads are present on all digits. Adult males are smaller than females and may have loose skin over their throat (which is inflated while they call).

Adult green treefrogs range in length from 32-57 mm (1¼-2¼ inches). The record size is 64 mm (2½ inches; Conant, 1975).

FIG. 50. Green Treefrog male "calling".

Habits and Habitat.—This species prefers permanent bodies of water, especially cattail marshes, cypress swamps, or river sloughs. Green treefrogs often spend the day resting among the long blades of cattails where they are well hidden by their light green color. They are active on warm nights, climbing among vegetation in search of insects.

Breeding.—Male green treefrogs may be heard in chorus from early May until early August, but egg laying probably occurs in June or early July (Garton and Brandon, 1975). Males call from plants, bushes, and trees along the water's edge, or while sitting on floating plants. They begin calling after dark, and may continue until just before midnight. Amplexus will only occur when a female approaches and actually touches a calling male (Fig. 51). A female may lay between 500-1,000 eggs. The eggs are fertilized by the male as they are released by the female, and are laid near the water's surface on floating vegetation. Hatching takes place in two to three days and transformation to froglets occurs between late June and early September (Garton and Brandon, 1975).

Fig. 51. A pair of Green Treefrogs in amplexus (male is on top).

The call of a male green treefrog is a series of measured nasal *"quank, quank, quank"* sounds with a ringing or metallic character.

Remarks.—Populations of green treefrogs in Missouri represent the northwest limit of the total range of this species. Swamp and marsh draining, and channelization of streams in southeastern Missouri have destroyed a large part of the suitable habitat of this species. Large areas of swamps and marshes should be preserved so that this species can remain a part of the natural wildlife heritage of Missouri.

Missouri Distribution.—The green treefrog is restricted to the extreme southeastern corner of Missouri and is associated with the cypress swamps and marshes which were once abundant in that area of the state.

FIG. 52. Adult Northern Spring Peeper, *Hyla crucifer crucifer.*

NORTHERN SPRING PEEPER
Hyla crucifer crucifer Wied

Description.—A small pinkish or light tan treefrog with a dark X-mark on the back. General coloration may vary from pink to tan, light brown, or gray. The dark X-mark may be very faint in light colored individuals or prominent in darker frogs. There is a dark line running across the top of the head, between the eyes, and dark bars are found on the legs. The belly is a plain cream color. The tips of the fingers and toes all have distinct adhesive pads. Males can be distinguished from females by their smaller size, and during the breeding season, by their darker throats.

The northern spring peeper ranges in length from 19-32 mm (¾-1¼ inches). The record is 35 mm (1⅜ inches; Conant, 1975).

Habits and Habitat.—This is primarily a woodland species, living near ponds, streams or swamps where there is thick undergrowth. The northern spring peeper usually remains hidden during the day, becoming active at dusk; however, it may become active during the day if heavy rains persist. This species is active from early spring to late fall in Missouri. A variety of small insects are eaten.

Breeding.—The northern spring peeper breeds in early spring, usually from early March to late May in Missouri. Temporary ponds or semi-permanent swamps are their favorite breeding sites, especially if brush, branches, and rooted plants are standing in the water. The males emit their calls from sites at the edge of the water or from branches of trees which are standing in the water. While in amplexus, the female will lay up to several hundred eggs which are fertilized by the male as they are laid. The eggs are laid singly and are attached to floating plants and sticks in the water. They hatch in three to four days, and metamorphose in about three months.

The call of the male northern spring peeper is a clear, high pitched peep, with a slight rise at the end. The peeping call is repeated about one per second (Conant, 1975). This frog is one of the first species to begin calling in the spring, and choruses may be heard from any temporary pond or swamp. After the breeding

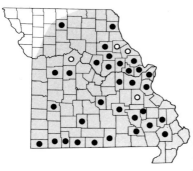

season the call may be heard during the day or night from wooded areas. Smith (1961) reported that males may be heard calling in the autumn in Illinois. Johnson (1975) heard several choruses of northern spring peepers calling on a November night in eastern Missouri.

Missouri Distribution.—The northern spring peeper is found throughout Missouri with the exception of the extreme northwestern corner.

FIG. 53. Adult Eastern Gray Treefrog, *Hyla versicolor.*

GRAY TREEFROG
Hyla versicolor—chrysoscelis Complex

Description.—In external appearance, both species in this complex can be described together. The gray treefrog is a fairly large tree-frog, with prominent adhesive pads on fingers and toes and rough skin. Coloration of an individual is quite variable, from green to light greenish-gray, gray, brown, or dark brown. Except for very light individuals, a few large, irregularly shaped dark blotches are usually present on the back. The belly is white. A large white spot is always present below each eye. Yellow or orange-yellow color-ation is found on the inside of the hind legs. Both species of gray treefrogs found in Missouri are morphologically indistinguishable. During the breeding season, females usually appear more heavy-bodied, while males have dark throats.

Adult gray treefrogs range in length from 32-51 mm (1¼-2 inches). The record is 60 mm (2⅜ inches; Conant, 1975).

Habits and Habitat.—These look-alike species of treefrogs appear to have the same habits and habitat preference in Missouri. Gray treefrogs live in woodlands where they spend most of their time in trees. During the breeding season they may be seen on the ground at night enroute to a breeding pond or pool. These breeding sites may be permanent or semi-permanent woodland ponds, swamps, ditches, or river sloughs. During the day they take refuge beneath or on rough tree bark where their color pattern blends perfectly. Gray treefrogs feed on various arboreal insects.

FIG. 54. Eastern Gray Treefrog male "calling".

Breeding.—In Missouri, gray treefrogs breed from early April to early June. Males gather and begin calling at breeding sites when the night air temperature is 60°F or more. They may sit at the water's edge or station themselves on a log or branch above the water. A male will grasp a female with his front legs when she comes near him. As they float in the water the female will begin laying eggs. She may lay up to 1,800 eggs, which are fertilized by the male as they are laid. The eggs are laid in clumps of 30-40 eggs and are attached to floating vegetation. Hatching takes place four to five days later, and the tadpoles transform into froglets in about two months (Collins, 1974).

Calls of the two gray treefrogs found in Missouri are described in the *Remarks* section of this account. Males may be heard calling away from breeding sites until early October.

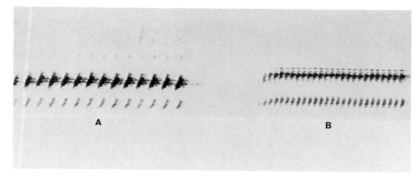

Fɪɢ. 55. Sonogram of *Hyla versicolor* (A) 19 pulses/sec; and *H. chrysoscelis* (B) 42 pulses/sec. Recorded May 5, 1975, 2 miles N. Higginsville, La-Fayette Co., Mo. The two species were calling sympatrically at an air temp. of 22.2°C. Recording analyzed with a Kay model 6061A Sono-Graph (narrow band), by L. E. Brown and R. S. Funk (Ill. State Univ.).

Remarks.—The eastern gray treefrog *(Hyla versicolor)*, and Cope's gray treefrog *(Hyla chrysoscelis)*, can be distinguished in the field by comparing the calls of the males. In *Hyla versicolor*, the call is a musical, bird-like trill, which may vary from 17-35 pulses per second (depending on the frog's temperature). The call of *Hyla chrysoscelis* may be described as a high pitched buzzing trill, with from 34-69 pulses per second depending on the frog's temperature (Fig. 55). For proper identification of gray treefrog calls, a tape recording of the call must be analyzed in the laboratory and the results correlated with the treefrog's temperature when recorded. Another difference between these two treefrogs is the number of chromosomes: tetraploid in *Hyla versicolor;* and diploid in *Hyla chrysoscelis*. In addition, the red blood cells of *Hyla versicolor* are larger than those of *Hyla chrysoscelis*. Johnson (1966) reported that the two gray treefrog species were genetically incompatible throughout their distribution.

Missouri Distribution.—Both species of gray treefrogs have been

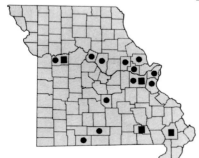

recorded in Missouri (dots are *H. versicolor*, squares are *H. chryso-scelis*) but not enough data have been accumulated to show precise geographic separation. County records of museum specimens collected in Missouri could not be used because they are not identifiable to species. I have found both species sympatrically in several Missouri locations. It is apparent that much field work is needed in order to better understand the distribution of the two gray treefrogs in Missouri.

Fig. 56. Adult Illinois Chorus Frog, *Pseudacris streckeri illinoensis*.

ILLINOIS CHORUS FROG
Pseudacris streckeri illinoensis Smith

Description.—A medium sized member of the treefrog family although it has little resemblance to a treefrog. This frog is chubby in appearance, and the fore legs are large and muscular, almost toad-like. The general ground color may vary from a light tan to a tannish-gray. There is a distinct V-shaped mark between the eyes, a dark stripe from the snout to the shoulder, and a dark spot below the eyes. A pair of large V-shaped dark markings will usually be found on the back behind the head. These markings are dark gray to brownish-gray in color. The skin is rough or granulated. The belly is white. Webbing of the hind feet is poorly developed.

Adult Illinois chorus frogs range in length from 25-41 mm (1-1⅝ inches). The record is 48 mm (1⅞ inches; Conant, 1975).

Habits and Habitat.—This frog prefers flat sandy areas in Missouri and makes its home in the cotton and bean fields of the southeastern corner of the state. Because it spends so much time buried in loose sandy soil, little is known about its habits outside the breeding season. These frogs enter the soil head first using their strong front legs and hands for digging (Brown *et al.*, 1972). Their strong hands seem to have good grasping ability, and I have observed them hanging onto grasses as they sit in the water during the breeding season.

This species eats various small insects and possibly burrowing insect larvae.

Breeding.—The Illinois chorus frog breeds early and, depending on local weather conditions, may begin in late February or early March and last until early April. Usual breeding sites are flooded cotton fields, ditches, or other temporary bodies of water. The males can be seen calling while floating in the water, sitting on some floating grass, or sitting along the edge of the water. A male will clasp a female about mid-body and, while they are floating in shallow water, the female will begin laying 200-400 eggs. Females may be observed using their hands to grasp onto twigs or grass for support. As the female lays the eggs they are fertilized by the male. Once the eggs have hatched, the tadpoles will take up to 60 days to transform into froglets. Smith (1961) reported that newly metamorphosed Illinois chorus frogs are dull gray in color and have inconspicuous markings.

The call of the male Illinois chorus frog is a clear, quick series of high pitched bird-like whistles.

Remarks.—Although this species still exists in the highly cultivated area of southeastern Missouri, it may not be able to withstand the wide use of fertilizers, herbicides, and insecticides that are dumped onto its habitat year after year.

Missouri Distribution.—The Illinois chorus frog is restricted to the southeastern corner of Missouri.

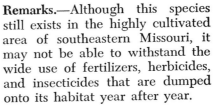

Fɪɢ. 57. Adult Western Chorus Frog, *Pseudacris triseriata triseriata.*

WESTERN CHORUS FROG
Pseudacris triseriata (Wied)

Description.—A small gray or brownish-gray frog with three dark stripes down the back. The upper lip is white. There is another dark brown or black stripe extending from the snout through the eye, and down the side to the groin. The head, body, and legs may be gray, tan, or brown. The three dark stripes on the back may be broad and continuous from head to back legs, or they may be broken into three rows of spots. A dark triangle is usually found on the head between the eyes. The dark markings on the back and legs may be dark gray or brown. The belly is white and there may be a few gray spots on the throat and chest. Adult females are larger than males, and during the breeding season the males have dark throats.

Adult western chorus frogs range in length from 19-38 mm (¾-1½ inches; Conant, 1975).

Habits and Habitat.—This frog seems most abundant in grasslands, but has also been found in agricultural areas. Other habitats include damp woods along ditches and streams or near farm ponds, and at the edges of marshes. Because they can take shelter in animal burrows, under logs or rocks, or in loose soil, they are seldom seen after the breeding season. Breeding sites are generally temporary bodies of water: flooded corn fields, ditches, woodland pools, or river sloughs. In Missouri, the western chorus frog probably is the first frog to become active in the spring. This species eats a variety of small insects and insect larvae.

Breeding.—Western chorus frogs begin breeding activities in late February or early March in Missouri, with peak activity during April. A chorus of males has been heard calling at temperatures as low as 35°F (Collins, 1974). A male will clasp a female behind her front legs, and while they are in amplexus, she will lay from 500-1,500 eggs. The eggs are fertilized by the male as they are laid and become attached to submerged grasses in clutches containing from 20-300 eggs. Hatching takes place in a few days, and the tadpoles will begin to metamorphose one to two months later (Collins, 1974).

The call of the male western chorus frog is a vibrating *"prrrreep"* with a rise in pitch at the end, and lasting one to two seconds. The sound may be similar to running a fingernail over the small teeth of a pocket comb (Conant, 1975).

Subspecies.—Two subspecies of chorus frogs occur in Missouri. The western chorus frog, *Pseudacris triseriata triseriata* (Wied), described above, and the upland chorus frog, *Pseudacris triseriata feriarum* (Baird). In the latter, the size, body color, and shape are like *P. t. triseriata*, but the dark stripes on the back are generally narrow or are broken up into three rows of spots. These markings may be rather faint on some individuals. The stripe along the side tends to be dark gray rather than black. The breeding habits are the same, but the upland chorus frog seems to prefer a more wooded habitat such as swamps, moist woods, and edges of marshes.

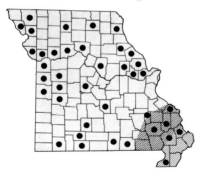

Due to the large amount of variation in both *Pseudacris t. triseriata* and *P. t. feriarum,* it is difficult to distinguish the two forms when examining specimens from southeastern Missouri. A large area of intergradation seems to occur in that part of the state.

Missouri Distribution.—The western chorus frog (stippling) is found state-wide except in southeastern Missouri where it intergrades with and is subsequently replaced by the upland chorus frog (hatch lines).

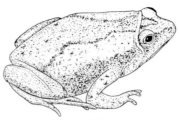

Fig. 58. Eastern Narrow-mouthed Toad, *Gastrophryne carolinensis.*

FAMILY MICROHYLIDAE
NARROW-MOUTHED TOADS

This large family of burrowing, secretive, frogs has representatives in Asia, Africa, Northern Australia, New Guinea, Madagascar, North and South America. The group probably originated in Asia. The family contains 55 genera and over 215 species. In the United States this group is represented by 2 genera and 3 species; of these, two species of one genus *(Gastrophryne)* are found in Missouri. Most members of this group are fossorial, spending a great part of their time in burrows or under rocks or logs. They tend to be small, plump, and squatty in appearance. All species found in the United States have a characteristic fold of skin behind a small, narrow, pointed head. Although many types of small insects may be eaten, these amphibians are mostly anteaters.

Fɪɢ. 59. Adult Eastern Narrow-mouthed Toad, *Gastrophryne carolinensis.*

EASTERN NARROW-MOUTHED TOAD
Gastrophryne carolinensis (Holbrook)

Description.—A small, plump frog with a fold of skin behind its narrow, pointed head. General coloration may be tan, brown, or reddish-brown. The color pattern on the back forms a long dark wedge with the narrow end at the head. This dark wedge is bordered by a wide lateral stripe of lighter color. There is also a dark stripe running from the snout along the side to the hind legs. Much of this pattern may be obscured by the presence of numerous small, irregular dark brown or black markings. The belly is mottled with dark gray. The small, pointed head, a fold of skin across the back of the head, short legs, and absence of both an external eardrum (tympanum) and webbing between the toes, are all characteristics of this burrowing frog. Males can be distinguished from females by their deeply pigmented throat.

Adult eastern narrow-mouthed toads range in length from 22-32 mm (⅞-1¼ inches). The record is 38 mm (1½ inches; Conant, 1975).

Habits and Habitat.—This frog spends most of its time in loose damp soil under rocks, logs, or boards. It prefers a habitat where shelter and moist soil are available, usually in the vicinity of ponds and streams. However, in the Ozarks, specimens have been found under flat rocks in relatively dry cedar glades. Once an eastern narrow-mouthed toad is uncovered, it tries to escape with a series of quick hops and a scramble into leaf litter or nearby hiding place. The primary food of this species is ants, although termites and small beetles are also eaten.

Breeding.—The eastern narrow-mouthed toad selects permanent or semi-permanent bodies of water in which to breed, including ponds, lakes, swamps, or ditches. In Missouri choruses of males are not usually heard until late May or June. The males stay in hiding as they call, usually under leaves or other debris at the water's edge. Once a male has attracted a female, he will clasp her with his front legs and may continue to call during amplexus. Special glands on the belly of the male secrete a substance which causes the male and female to become firmly stuck together. It is possible that these special "breeding glands" evolved in the eastern narrow-mouthed toads due to their rounded bodies and the male's short arms, which make amplexus difficult (Conway and Metter, 1967).

The female will lay up to 850 eggs (Wright and Wright, 1949) in a film at the surface and these are fertilized by the male as they are laid. The eggs hatch quickly, in less than two days, and the tadpoles metamorphose 30-60 days later.

The call of male eastern narrow-mouthed toads is a bleating nasal *"baaaaa"*, lasting from one to four seconds, sounding like the cry of a forlorn lamb.

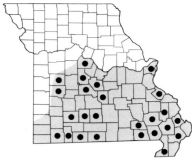

Remarks.—In western Missouri this species is known to occur in sympatry with the Great Plains narrow-mouthed toad, *Gastrophryne olivacea* (see *G. olivacea* account for ways to distinguish the two species, and for a discussion on possible hybridization).

Missouri Distribution.—The eastern narrow-mouthed toad is found in the southern half of Missouri.

FIG. 60. Adult Great Plains Narrow-mouthed Toad, *Gastrophryne olivacea.*

GREAT PLAINS NARROW-MOUTHED TOAD
Gastrophryne olivacea (Hallowell)

Description.—This small toad can be identified by its plump body, small pointed head, a fold of skin across the back of the head, short legs, and uniform coloration. The general coloration is gray, tan, or olive-tan. Small black spots may be scattered over the back and hind legs. There is no webbing between the toes. The belly is white. Adult females are larger than males and during the breeding season the males have dark throats.

This species can best be distinguished from the eastern narrow-mouthed toad by its overall lighter coloration and the absence of any prominent dorsal markings.

Adult Great Plains narrow-mouthed toads range in length from 22-38 mm (⅞-1½ inches). The record is 41 mm (1⅝ inches; Conant, 1975).

Habits and Habitat.—This species prefers grasslands, rocky and wooded hills, and areas along the edge of marshes. These frogs spend most of their time hiding in loose soil, under rocks, boards, logs, or other objects, and have been known to take shelter in animal burrows (Blair, 1936). This species has evolved a toxic skin secretion which may protect it from ant bites, since it is known to sit on ant hills while eating its preferred food.

Breeding.—Usual breeding sites are temporary ponds in flooded fields, pools in wooded areas, or ditches. Warm, heavy rains will stimulate males to congregate at breeding sites and begin calling. A male clasps a female just behind her front legs. Special skin glands on the male's belly secrete a glue-like substance which helps hold them together (Fitch, 1956; Conway and Metter, 1967). During amplexus the female lays over 600 eggs and the male fertilizes the eggs as they are laid. The eggs hatch in two to three days, and the tadpoles metamorphose between 20-30 days later (Collins, 1974). In Missouri, breeding may take place from late May to early July.

The call of a male Great Plains narrow-mouthed toad is a high pitched short *"peet"* followed by a nasal buzz, which lasts from one to four seconds. It may sound somewhat like the buzz of an angry bee (Conant, 1975).

Remarks.—Both *Gastrophryne carolinensis* and *G. olivacea* are known to occur together in several western counties in Missouri.

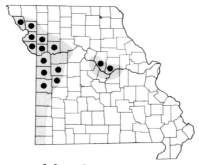

Sympatric populations and hybrids may be found in that area. However, the calls of both species are different enough to keep the populations isolated from excessive hybridization (Nelson, 1972).

Missouri Distribution.—The Great Plains narrow-mouthed toad has been reported from counties primarily in northwestern and western Missouri. Metter, *et al.* (1970) reported breeding populations in Boone and Calloway counties in central Missouri.

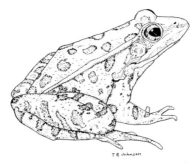

Fig. 61. Southern Leopard Frog, *Rana sphenocephala.*

FAMILY RANIDAE
TRUE FROGS

The family Ranidae is the largest and the most widespread family of frogs. It contains over 700 species in 37 genera, and probably had its origin in Africa. Representatives of this cosmopolitan family are found on nearly every major land mass, with the exception of New Zealand, central and southern Australia, and southern South America. The largest genus in the family is *Rana,* with over 250 species, and is the only genus of this family which is found in the United States, where 17 species occur. In Missouri the genus is represented by 7 species. Members of this family are commonly called "true frogs," and they are typically of medium to large size, have long legs, smooth skin, and webbing between the toes. Another common characteristic is a glandular *dorsolateral* fold or ridge of skin along each side of the back. The largest member of the group in the United States, the bullfrog *(Rana catesbeiana),* does not have this ridge of skin.

Natural food of the true frogs consists of nearly any animal small enough to be swallowed. Insects, spiders, crawfish, other frogs, fish, earthworms, etc., are consumed. The tadpoles of most species are herbivorous, with the exception of the wood frog *(Rana sylvatica),* which is carnivorous.

Fig. 62. Adult Northern Crawfish Frog, *Rana areolata circulosa*.

Northern Crawfish Frog
Rana areolata circulosa Davis and Rice

Description.—This is a medium-sized frog with a light ground color and numerous, closely set dark spots. The head is disproportionately large in this species. A prominent dorsolateral fold extends from the eye to the thigh. Ground color may vary from light tan to light gray, and the dark spots may be dark brown or gray, sometimes edged with white. Usually between the dark spots there is a fine network pattern or spotting of dark pigment. The belly is white. Males can be distinguished from females by their smaller size, enlarged thumbs, and presence (during the breeding season) of a pair of sac-like vocal pouches behind and below each eardrum (*tympanum*).

The northern crawfish frog ranges in length from 65-104 mm (2½-4 inches). The record is 114 mm (4½ inches; Conant, 1975).

Habits and Habitat.—In Missouri the northern crawfish frog is restricted to prairie or former prairie areas. Populations may be found in or near low lying meadows and pasture lands, as well as river flood plains. Although nearly all of the true prairie regions of Missouri have undergone intensive cultivation, this species has been able to survive.

Crawfish frogs are known to use crawfish burrows for retreats but may use burrows of other animals as well. A crawfish burrow being used by this frog will have a noticeably flattened platform at the entrance. Because the burrows may run from three to five feet deep, the frogs are probably able to use them as a winter retreat (Collins, 1974).

This is a very secretive species, spending most of its time hidden in burrows or under logs or boards. It is seldom encountered except during its short breeding season.

Food of this species consists of a variety of invertebrates, including small crawfish.

Breeding.—Northern crawfish frogs breed from March to early May. Males congregate in flooded fields, ditches, and farm ponds. Heavy rains and moderate temperatures seem to stimulate the males to chorus. Soon after the males begin to call, the egg-laden females begin to arrive at the breeding sites. A male will clasp a female behind her front legs and while in amplexus, the eggs are laid and fertilized by the male in the water. One female may lay up to 7,000 eggs (Collins, 1974). The eggs take a few days to hatch, and the tadpoles metamorphose in June or early July.

The call of a male northern crawfish frog may be described as a deep, loud, snoring "*gwaaaa*", which may be heard for a considerable distance. A number of males calling in chorus may sound like pigs during feeding time (Conant, 1975). The males will call while floating in open water, and have also been known to call while submerged in the water (Barbour, 1971).

Remarks.—This species is known to be common in a number of

prairie counties in Missouri. However, lowering of the water table and further alterations of optimal habitat by dams and levees, as well as stream channelization may have a detrimental effect on populations of the northern crawfish frog in our state.

Missouri Distribution.—This species occurs in the rather flat or rolling hills or prairies in western, central, and eastern Missouri.

FIG. 63. Adult Plains Leopard Frog, *Rana blairi.*

PLAINS LEOPARD FROG
Rana blairi Mecham, Littlejohn, Oldham, Brown, and Brown

Description.—A medium sized frog with light tan ground color and numerous rounded spots on the back. The head is rather wide and blunt, giving this species a stocky appearance. There is always a distinct light line along the upper jaw. A white spot is usually present on the tympanum. The dorsolateral folds are broken near the groin and a small posterior section of it is displaced further up toward the midline. The numerous brownish spots on the back and sides are usually circular, though always uniform in shape. A dark spot is usually present on the snout. The belly is white with some yellow coloration near the groin and on the lower thighs. This species can be distinguished from the southern leopard frog *(Rana sphenocephala)*, by the absence of any green coloration on the back, the rather blunt snout, broken and displaced section of the dorsolateral fold, and by the numerous rounded dorsal spots. (See southern leopard frog account). Male plains leopard frogs differ from females in having enlarged thumbs and small vocal sacs on each side of the head during the breeding season.

Adults of this species range in length from 51-95 mm (2-3¾ inches). The record is 111 mm (4⅜ inches; Conant, 1975).

Habits and Habitat.—This species is restricted to the grasslands of the Midwest. In Missouri, it can be found in the flatlands or rolling hills of the western and northern parts of the state where it lives near farm ponds, wet meadows, and along streams. It may venture into grassy areas at night or during wet weather.

These frogs will generally retreat into the mud and dead leaves at the bottom of ponds and streams during winter. The plains leopard frog eats a variety of insects.

Breeding.—This species breeds from late March to early May. Farm ponds, temporary pools, and marshes are preferred breeding sites. Males will gather at ponds and begin calling after sunset, especially after spring rains. Females are attracted by the male's call, and amplexus takes place in the water. The male clasps the female behind her front legs. Females lay from 4,000 to 6,500 eggs (Collins, 1974) in large clusters or spheres from three to six inches across (Smith, 1961). As the eggs are laid they are fertilized by the male. The eggs may hatch from a few days to nearly a week after being laid. Tadpole metamorphosis occurs in July or August. This species breeds slightly later in the spring than the southern leopard frog, *Rana sphenocephala* (Funk, *pers. comm.*). In some years, plains leopard frogs may breed during the autumn.

The call of the male plains leopard frog can be described as a rapid series of guttural "*chuck-chuck-chuck*" sounds at a pulse rate of five per second (Mecham *et al.*, 1973).

Remarks.—The plains leopard frog is known to occur sympatrically with the southern leopard frog *(R. sphenocephala)* in a number of

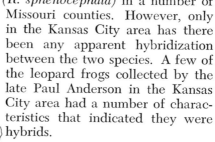

Missouri counties. However, only in the Kansas City area has there been any apparent hybridization between the two species. A few of the leopard frogs collected by the late Paul Anderson in the Kansas City area had a number of characteristics that indicated they were hybrids.

Missouri Distribution.—The plains leopard frog occurs throughout most of the northern half of Missouri.

FIG. 64. Adult Bullfrog, *Rana catesbeiana.*

BULLFROG
Rana catesbeiana (Shaw)

Description.—This is Missouri's largest frog. General coloration ranges from green to olive to brown. Some dark markings may be present on the back in the form of small brown spots or indistinct irregular blotches. The hind legs are heavily marked with dark brown bars. The belly is white with some yellow on the throat and gray mottling may be present. The external eardrum *(tympanum)* is large and round. Bullfrogs lack dorsolateral folds. Adult male bullfrogs have an eardrum much larger than the eye, which distinguishes them from females.

Adult bullfrogs range in length from 90-150 mm (3½-6 inches) snout-vent length. The record is 203 mm (8 inches; Conant, 1975).

Habits and Habitat.—This is Missouri's most aquatic species of frog. Bullfrogs spend most of their time in or very near aquatic habitats such as lakes, ponds, rivers, large creeks, sloughs, and permanent swamps or marshes. They may enter caves at times. A bullfrog was observed in a cave in eastern Missouri (Pingleton, Roth and Rogers, 1975).

The bullfrog is easily disturbed during the day and escapes by powerful jumps into the water. However, it can be approached more easily at night with the aid of a flash light. In Missouri adults of this species usually enter winter retreats in late October, and young bullfrogs follow a few weeks later (Willis, Moyle, and Baskett, 1956). They burrow into the mud at the bottom of rivers or ponds to avoid winter temperatures (Collins, 1974).

Crawfish, insects, other frogs, small snakes, fish and worms are some of the more common food animals eaten by bullfrogs. Their voracious appetite and size allow them to eat nearly any animal small enough to be captured and swallowed.

Breeding.—Adult bullfrogs begin to emerge from winter retreats in late March when surface water temperatures are about 55°F (Willis, *et al.*, 1956). However, male bullfrogs do not call until early April, and choruses are first heard in mid-May. The peak of breeding activity takes place the last week of June and quickly tapers off during early July.

In Missouri, female bullfrogs become sexually mature between 123-125 mm (4.8-4.9 inches) snout-vent length (Willis *et al.*, 1956), while males attain sexual maturity at about 120 mm (4.7 inches) snout-vent length (Schroeder, 1975).

During breeding, a male will mount a female and begin amplexus, holding onto the female just behind her front legs. As the female begins to lay her eggs (which may number between 10,000-20,000) they are fertilized by the male. The eggs are laid as a large, wide mass near the surface of the water. The eggs hatch in four to five days (Collins, 1974) and, in Missouri, the large tadpoles will usually metamorphose in 11-14 months (Willis *et al.*, 1956). Once metamorphosis take place, it may take an additional two to three years before adult size is reached (Barbour, 1971).

The call of a male bullfrog can be described as a deep sonorous *"ger-a-a-rum"*, which may carry for a distance of half a mile or more. Males may be heard calling during the day, but most vocalization takes place at night.

Remarks.—The bullfrog is classified as a game animal by the Missouri Department of Conservation and is protected under the state's wildlife code. A person holding a valid fishing permit can capture and possess up to 8 bullfrogs between June 30 and November 30. The legs of bullfrogs are edible and considered by many people to be a delicacy.

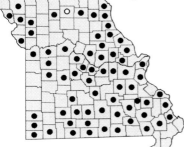

Missouri Distribution.—This familiar amphibian is found throughout Missouri.

FIG. 65. Adult Green Frog, *Rana clamitans melanota.*

GREEN FROG
Rana clamitans Latreille

Description.—A medium sized frog. General coloration may vary from green to brown. The upper lip and head are usually green. Faint dark spots may be present on the back, and the legs may have indistinct dark spots or bars. The belly is white with some dusky markings on the sides. Adult males have a bright yellow throat. A distinct dorsolateral fold is always present, but extends only to mid-body, not to groin. Tympanum is large and conspicuous, larger than the eye in males. Males also have swollen thumbs and heavier front legs. This species may be confused with the bullfrog, but is smaller and has a prominent dorsolateral fold, which bullfrogs lack.

Adult green frogs range in length from 57-89 mm (2¼-3½ inches). The record is 102 mm (4 inches; Conant, 1975).

Habits and Habitat.—In Missouri this species is more apt to be found in creeks and streams, especially in the Ozarks. Other habitats may include ponds, rivers, and sloughs. It is a rather solitary animal, and will quickly jump into the water when alarmed, often emitting a high-pitched squawk as it jumps (Smith, 1961).

This amphibian has been studied very little in Missouri. It presumably eats a variety of insects and small crawfish.

Breeding.—The reproductive biology of this frog has not been studied in the state. Generally speaking, the green frog may breed from late May until late August, but June is probably the peak breeding month. Any permanent standing water may be used as a breeding site, including ponds, swamps and sloughs. Once a male has engaged a female in amplexus, the female will begin depositing her eggs, which may number 4,000, (Wright and Wright, 1949) in a wide, floating mass on the surface of the water. The small tadpoles begin hatching in several days, depending on water temperature, but metamorphosis will not occur until the following summer (Smith, 1961).

The call of a male green frog can be described as an explosive "*bong*", sounding like a loose banjo string. The sound may be emitted once, or repeated three to four times (Conant, 1975).

Subspecies.—Missouri has two subspecies of *Rana clamitans*. The green frog, *Rana clamitans melanota* (Rafinesque), which was described in detail in the above account. The other subspecies, *Rana clamitans clamitans* Latreille, known as the bronze frog, is not common in Missouri. It can be distinguished from the green frog by its smaller size, 54-76 mm (2⅛-3 inches), by its more brown or bronze colored body, and by the lack of green coloration on the upper lip and head. The bronze frog may also have more distinct dark markings on back and limbs.

Remarks.—In Missouri, these two frogs are often misidentified as young bullfrogs. Make sure to check whether the frog in question has a dorsolateral fold. Green frogs and bronze frogs have them; bullfrogs do not.

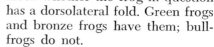

Missouri Distribution.—The green frog (stippling) is found over most of Missouri with the exception of the northwestern part of the state. The bronze frog (hatch lines) is known only from extreme southeastern Missouri, and intergradation between the two subspecies occurs in several southeastern counties.

Fig. 66. Adult Pickerel Frog, *Rana palustris.*

PICKEREL FROG
Rana palustris Le Conte

Description.—A medium sized frog with prominent dorsolateral folds and two parallel rows of squarish or rectangular spots running down the back between the folds. General coloration is tan or gray. A white line is present along the upper jaw. The dorsolateral fold is distinct, extending down to the groin. This fold may be white, cream, yellow, or gray in color. Spots on the back are reddish-brown, dark brown, or black. Dark bars on the hind legs are prominent. The underside of hind legs and groin area are washed with bright yellow, orange-yellow, or pinkish-yellow. The belly is white.

During the breeding season, males can be distinguished from females by their enlarged thumbs with dark, thick, pads. Adult males are generally smaller than adult females.

The pickerel frog may be confused with the two species of leopard frogs found in Missouri (*Rana blairi,* plains leopard frog, and *R. sphenocephala,* southern leopard frog), but the latter lack any bright yellow under the hind legs, and their dorsal spots are more rounded and scattered over the dorsum with no regular pattern.

Adult pickerel frogs may range in length from 44-76 mm (1¾-3 inches). The record is 87 mm (3 7/16 inches; Conant, 1975).

Habits and Habitat.—This species is usually associated with cold streams, springs, and cool, shaded woodland ponds. In Missouri, it is found abundantly in Ozark streams. These frogs may often be seen in the evening along the edges of shaded streams, or during the day under rocks along the water's edge. The pickerel frog is frequently found in the numerous caves of the Missouri Ozarks, though they seldom venture too far back from the twilight zone. However, they are not restricted to the Ozarks. They may also live along streams in grassland or pastures, or near farm ponds. Along the Mississippi River they are associated with springs and creeks which flow from limestone bluffs.

Little is known about the natural history of this frog in Missouri, but presumably, it consumes a variety of insects and other invertebrates.

Pickerel frogs probably use mud at the bottom of streams or ponds as winter retreats, or over-winter inside caves. Large numbers of pickerel frogs crowded together have been observed in Missouri caves during the winter.

Breeding.—Woodland ponds, sloughs or creeks, and even water filled ditches may be used as breeding sites. The breeding season has not been reported for Missouri populations, but in other states this species breeds from late March to early May (Barbour, 1971; Conant, 1975). Males will usually form a chorus at one end of a pond, where over a dozen may call from a relatively small area (Wright and Wright, 1949). Amplexus will take place as soon as a male is approached by a female. The eggs are fertilized as they are laid. The female lays the eggs in water in the form of globular masses, attached to submerged sticks or stems. A total of 2,000-3,000 eggs may be laid by each female (Wright and Wright, 1949). The small tadpoles begin hatching from the eggs in 10 days or more, depending on the water temperature, and will usually begin to metamorphose in three to three and one-half months. Pickerel frog tadpoles collected in late April in Pulaski County, and kept at 70°F, transformed into froglets by mid-July.

The call of a male pickerel frog may be described as a continued low-pitched snore lasting one to two seconds (Conant, 1975). A number of authors have reported this frog vocalizing while under water (Morris, 1944; Wright and Wright, 1949; Barbour, 1971; Conant, 1975).

Remarks.—Skin secretions of the pickerel frog have been reported 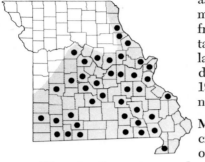 as harsh or even toxic to small animals. If newly captured pickerel frogs are placed in the same container with other frog species, the latter will die within a short time due to these skin secretions (Morris, 1944). Most frog-eating snakes will not eat pickerel frogs.

Missouri Distribution.—This species is common in the southern half of Missouri and along the Mississippi River in the eastern and northeastern parts of the state.

FIG. 67. Adult Southern Leopard Frog, *Rana sphenocephala*.

SOUTHERN LEOPARD FROG
Rana sphenocephala Cope

Description.—A medium sized frog with a variable number of rounded or oblong dark spots on the back. The dorsolateral fold is distinct, yellow or tan in color, and extends to the groin. The head is somewhat long with a pointed snout. General coloration is green, greenish-brown, or brown. Normally at least some green coloration is present on the dorsum. A white spot is usually present in the center of the tympanum and a distinct white line occurs on the upper lip. Dark markings on the hind legs appear as broken bars or elongated spots. Normally no dark spot is present on the snout. The belly is white. Males can be distinguished from females during the breeding season by their smaller size, enlarged thumbs, and vocal sacs on the sides of the head.

The southern leopard frog can be distinguished from the plains leopard frog, *Rana blairi,* by having larger, fewer, and elongated dorsal spots, by the presence of green coloration on the dorsum, by the more elongated head and pointed snout, and by the dorsolateral fold (which extends unbroken or if broken not displaced, to the groin). In the pickerel frog, *Rana palustris,* the dorsal spots are squarish or rectangular and set in two uniform rows down the back. Pickerel frogs have some bright yellow under the hind legs and groin. This coloration is lacking in leopard frogs.

Adult southern leopard frogs range from 51-89 mm (2-3½ inches) in snout-vent length. The record length is 127 mm (5 inches; Conant, 1975).

Habits and Habitat.—This species utilizes a wide variety of aquatic habitats including marshes, swamps, ponds, lakes, sloughs, rivers, and creeks. During summer, the southern leopard frog may venture far from water into pastures, meadows, or wooded areas. When near an aquatic habitat, these frogs sit at the water's edge, but quickly enter the water with a powerful jump if alarmed. A wide variety of insects and other invertebrates are eaten by this species.

Breeding.—In Missouri, the southern leopard frog breeds from mid-March to early May. Ponds, sloughs, and flooded ditches are used as breeding sites. Males will call while floating in the water, or more often will hide themselves among grasses, stems, etc., in shallow water. Once a male has grasped a female, amplexus begins. As the female lays her eggs in the water they are fertilized by the male. From 3,000-5,000 eggs are normally laid (Smith, 1961) in several round clumps or masses. Hatching takes about a week, depending on water temperature, and the tadpoles metamorphose from mid-June to mid-August. In some years, southern leopard frogs may breed during the autumn.

The call of the male southern leopard frog can be described as a series of abrupt, chuckle-like *"quacking"* sounds, repeated at a rate of 12 pulses per second (Illinois population, Mecham *et al.,* 1973).

Remarks.—In her work on the systematics of leopard frogs of the United States, Pace (1974) used the specific name *utricularia* for the southern leopard frog. Subsequently, Conant (1975), following Pace's published use of the name, applied *utricularia* to the southern leopard frog. I have retained the old and more commonly used name, *sphenocephala*, for this species until the International Commission on Zoological Nomenclature decides which name should be used (Brown, Smith and Funk, 1977).

A great deal of field work is needed on the leopard frogs in Missouri. Funk (1975) reported this species sympatric with *R. blairi* in Howard County. I have examined specimens of both species found sympatrically in Jackson and Montgomery counties. Calls, time of breeding, breeding site preference, habitat preference, and

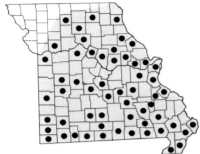

egg and tadpole identification are some of the important factors which should be investigated in areas where the two species are found together.

Missouri Distribution.—The southern leopard frog has been found throughout most of Missouri, except the northwestern part of the state. Conant (1975) inadvertently neglected to show this species occurring in central Missouri.

Fig. 68. Adult Wood Frog, *Rana sylvatica.*

Wood Frog
Rana sylvatica Le Conte

Description.—The wood frog is small to medium sized, tan or brown in color, with a distinct dark brown "mask" on the side of the head that extends from the snout to behind the tympanum. General coloration varies from pinkish-tan, light brown, reddish-brown, to dark brown. Scattered small dark brown markings may be present on the dorsum, and the hind legs usually have dark longitudinal bars. There is a prominent white line along the upper lip. The belly is white with scattered dusky markings. The dorsolateral fold is distinct and extends to the groin.

During the breeding season adult male wood frogs can be distinguished from females by their smaller size, darker color, enlarged thumbs, and vocal sacs found just above their front legs.

The only other frog found in Missouri which may be confused with the wood frog is the bronze frog which may have a brownish coloration similar to some wood frogs. However, no other frog in Missouri has the distinctive dark brown "mask" through the eye.

Adult Missouri wood frogs range from 45-60 mm (1½-2 5/16 inches) in length. The largest specimen collected in Missouri was 63 mm (2½ inches).

Habits and Habitat.—This species is normally associated with cool, moist woods. It may be encountered near woodland ponds, springs, or streams but is known to venture well away from bodies of water into wooded areas during the summer. The wood frog is a solitary animal and rather secretive. I have observed wood frogs from Wisconsin under logs on several occasions. Specific habits of this frog in Missouri are not known due to its extreme rarity in this state. Presumably, a variety of small insects and other invertebrates are eaten by this species.

Remarks.—This is an extremely rare amphibian in Missouri. Due to its low numbers, the Missouri Department of Conservation has classified the wood frog as an endangered species and accorded it complete protection.

Missouri Distribution.—The wood frog is known from only a few localities in Missouri. Those found in southwestern Missouri are

probably disjunct or relict populations. It is questionable whether any wood frogs still exist in the St. Louis area. The record for Dallas County has a question mark indicating a field observation reported to me, but no specimen was collected for validation. Conant (1975) indicated a record of this species in northeastern Missouri, but upon investigation, I found that the specimen (reportedly collected in Macon County) had been lost. Thus, this county record is also indicated with a question mark.

AMPHIBIAN SPECIES OF POSSIBLE OCCURRENCE IN MISSOURI

The following species or subspecies have populations which come within 25 miles of the Missouri state line (Conant, 1975). To date, no actual specimens of these amphibians have been collected within the boundaries of Missouri. Due to their close proximity, some may eventually be found in this state and thus, are briefly treated in this section. The dwarf salamander, previously reported from Missouri, is listed in this section due to the lack of additional specimens since it was first reported.

Spotted Dusky Salamander, *Desmognathus fuscus conanti* Rossman.—This species was reported by Smith (1961) to occur in small colonies in extreme southern Illinois. Conant (1975) showed its occurrence in extreme northeastern Arkansas (Crowley's Ridge area), but his map for this subspecies erroneously shows its distribution as southeastern Missouri (Easteria, *pers. comm.*).

Northern Two-Lined Salamander, *Eurycea bislineata bislineata* (Green); and **Southern Two-Lined Salamander,** *E. b. cirrigera* (Green).—Both forms of two-lined salamanders are shown by Conant (1975) to range into southeastern Illinois *(E. b. bislineata)*, and into western Kentucky and Tennessee *(E. b. cirrigera)*.

Dwarf Salamander, *Eurycea quadridigitatus* (Holbrook).—Since Anderson's (1945) published record of two dwarf salamanders from Berry County, Missouri, no additional specimens have been found in the state. I have confirmed the identity of both specimens collected from Missouri. Mittleman (1967) showed the Missouri locality of this salamander and remarked that the populations of this species in Arkansas and Missouri are "possibly disjunct." Conant (1975) also mapped this southwestern Missouri record. Because the record has not been substantiated by more recent collecting and until further evidence indicates otherwise, the dwarf salamander is not recognized as a part of the herpetofauna of Missouri and is reported here as possibly occurring in the southwestern corner of the state.

Hurter's Spadefoot Toad, *Scaphiopus holbrookii hurterii* Strecker.—This western subspecies of the spadefoot toad has been shown by both Wasserman (1968) and Conant (1975) to range into the extreme southwestern Missouri. Collins (1974) reported that no specimens of this subspecies have been reported from the adjacent area of southeastern Kansas. To date, the Hurter's spadefoot toad has not been located in Missouri.

Western Bird-Voiced Treefrog, *Hyla avivoca avivoca* Viosca.—This beautiful little treefrog has been reported in southern Illinois (Smith, 1961 and 1968; Conant, 1975), western Kentucky (Barbour, 1971; Conant, 1975), and northwestern Arkansas (Turnipseed, 1976). Many attempts to locate this species in the remaining swamps of southeastern Missouri have failed. After much field work in that area, Smith (1966a) doubted that this species occurs in Missouri.

Northern Leopard Frog, *Rana pipiens* Schreber.—Smith (1961),

Pace (1974), and Conant (1975) report the northern leopard frog in western counties of Illinois near the northeastern corner of Missouri. Pace (1974), Conant (1975), and Kruse and Dunlap (1976) reported that this species ranges into the southeastern corner of Nebraska, close to the northwestern corner of Missouri. Even though adequate habitat is not available for *R. pipiens* in northern Missouri, the chance exists that this species may someday be found there (Funk, 1975).

GLOSSARY

Amplexus—Sexual embrace of amphibians in which the male grasps the female's body from above with his forelimbs. This allows the eggs to be fertilized externally by the male as they are being laid by the female.

Boss—A swollen rounded area on the middle of the snout. Also called cranial boss.

Carnivorous—Consumption and digestion of other animals.

Cirri—Downward projections from the nostrils in males of certain lungless salamanders. The naso-labial groove extends downward to the tip of each cirrus.

Cloaca—The common chamber through which the urinary, digestive, and reproductive canals discharge their contents. Also called the vent or anus.

Costal groove—Vertical grooves located on the sides of the body between the front and hind limbs.

Cranial crests—Raised ridges on the head located between or behind the eyes.

Diurnal—Active during the day.

Dorsal—The upper surface or back of an animal.

Dorsolateral fold—A line of raised glandular skin along an area between the back and side.

Dorsum—The entire back of an animal.

Fossorial—Adapted for living underground.

Herbivorous—Consumption and digestion of plants.

Herpetology—The branch of science dealing with the study of amphibians and reptiles.

Larva—The aquatic, gilled young of salamanders (plural: Larvae).

Lateral—The side of an animal.

Mental Gland—A light colored swelling below the chin on males of several species of plethodontid salamanders (usually more apparent during the breeding season).

Metamorphosis—A morphological change from a larva to an adult with the loss of larval characteristics and the acquisition of adult characteristics.

Middorsal—The area in the center of the back.

Naso-labial groove—A groove extending downward from the nostril and across the lip in the lungless salamanders.

Neotenic—Sexually mature and able to reproduce, but retaining the larval form and habits.

Nocturnal—Active at night.

Paedogenetic—The condition of some salamanders to retain some larval characteristics and to gain the ability to reproduce.

Parotoid—Large, wart-like glands located behind each eye in toads.

Spermatophore—A gelatinous cone with a cap consisting of sperm. Secreted by male salamanders and picked up by the female with her cloacal lips. Once inside the female, the sperm fertilize the eggs.

Snout-vent length (S-V)—The measurement of an animal from the tip of nose to cloaca. Usual method of measuring toads and frogs.

Sympatric—When two or more species occupy the same geographic area.

Tadpole—The aquatic larva of toads and frogs. Gills are present but hidden behind a flap of skin. The stage of life between the egg and the tailless young adult.

Troglodytic—Adaptations for cave dwelling.

Type-locality—The location of collection for the specimen that was used for the first published description of that species.

Vent—See cloaca.

Ventral—The lower surface or belly of an animal.

Vermiculation—Coloration of dark color in a worm-like pattern.

BIBLIOGRAPHY
PART I. GENERAL WORKS

This list consists of publications which deal in a general manner with the species of amphibians included in this book, and is provided for those who wish to learn more about amphibians.

AGASSIZ, L.

1857. Contributions to the natural history of the United States of America. Little, Brown, and Co., Boston. Vol. 1-2, 452 pp.

ANDERSON, J. D.

1965. *Ambystoma annulatum* Cope Ringed salamander. Cat. Am. Amphib. Rept., 19.1-19.2.

1967a. *Ambystoma maculatum* (Shaw) Spotted salamander. Cat. Am. Amphib. Rept., 51.1-51.4.

1967b. *Ambystoma opacum* (Gravenhorst) Marbled salamander. Cat. Am. Amphib. Rept., 46.1-46.2.

1967c. *Ambystoma texanum* (Matthes) Small-mouthed salamander. Cat. Am. Amphib. Rept., 37.1-37.2.

ANDERSON, P. K.

1954. Studies in the ecology of the narrow-mouthed toad *Microhyla carolinensis carolinensis*. Tulane Stud. Zool., 2:13-38.

BARBOUR, R. W.

1971. Amphibians and reptiles of Kentucky. Univ. Ky. Press. Lexington, x+334 pp.

BARBOUR, R. W. and W. L. GAULT.

1952. Notes on the spadefoot toad, *Scaphiopus h. holbrookii*. Copeia, 1952:192.

BISHOP, S. C.

1944. A new neotenic plethodont salamander, with notes on related species. Copeia, 1944:1-5.

1947. Handbook of salamanders. The salamanders of the United States, of Canada, and of lower California. Comstock Pub. Co., Inc. Ithaca., xiv+555 pp.

BLAIR, W. F.

1936. A note on the ecology of *Microyla olivacea*. Copeia, 1936:115.

BLANCHARD, F. N.

1935. The sex ratio in the salamander *Hemidactylium scutatum* (Schlegel). Copeia, 1935:103.

BRAGG, A. N.

1936. The ecological distribution of some North American Anura. Am. Nat., 70:459-466.

1937. Observations of *Bufo cognatus* with special reference to breeding habits and eggs. Am. Midl. Nat., 18:273-284.

1940. Observations on the ecology and natural history of Anura. I. Habits, habitat and breeding of *Bufo cognatus* Say. Am. Nat., 74:322-349.

1942. Life history of Hurter's spadefoot. Anat. Rec., 84:506 (abstract).

1944. Breeding, habits, eggs, and tadpoles of *Scaphiopus hurterii*. Copeia, 1944:230-241.

1964. Further study of predation and cannibalism in spadefoot tadpoles. Herpetologica, 20:17-24.

BRANDON, R. A.

1961. A comparison of the larvae of five northern species of *Ambystoma* (Amphibia, Caudata). Copeia, 1961:377-383.

1970. *Typhlotriton* and *T. spelaeus*. Cat. Am. Amphib. Rept., 84.1-84.2.
BRANDON, R. A. and D. J. BREMER.
1966. Neotenic newts, *Notophthalmus viridescens louisianensis*, in southern Illinois. Herpetologica, 22:213-217.
BRANDON, R. A. and J. H. BLACK
1970. The taxonomic status of *Typhlotriton braggi*. (Caudata, Plethodontidae). Copeia, 1970:388-391.
BROWN, L. E.
1973. Speciation in the *Rana pipiens* complex. Am. Zool., 13:73-79.
BROWN, L. E. and J. R. BROWN.
1972a. Mating calls and distributional records of treefrogs of the *Hyla versicolor* complex in Illinois. J. Herp., 6:233-234.
1972b. Call types of the *Rana pipiens* complex in Illinois. Science, 176: 928-929.
BROWN, L. E., H. O. JACKSON and J. R. BROWN.
1972. Burrowing behavior of the chorus frog, *Pseudacris streckeri*. Herpetologica, 28:325-328.
BROWN, L. E., H. M. SMITH and R. S. FUNK.
1976. I.C.Z.N. to consider a proposal to conserve the name *Rana sphenocephala* Cope. Herp. Review, 7:5.
1977. Request for the conservation of *Rana sphenocephala* Cope 1886, and the suppression of *Rana utricularius* Harlan, 1826, and *Rana virescens* Cope, 1889 (Amphibia: Salientia). Bull. Zool. Nomen., 33:195-203.
BURT, C. E. and M. D. BURT.
1929. A collection of amphibians and reptiles from the Mississippi valley, with field observations. Am. Mus. Novitates, 381:1-14.
COCHRAN, D. M.
1961. Living amphibians of the world. Doubleday Co., Garden City, N.Y., 199 pp.
COLLINS, J. T.
1974. Amphibians and reptiles in Kansas. Univ. Kansas Mus. Nat. Hist. Publ. Ed. Ser., 1:1-283.
CONANT, R.
1958. A field guide to reptiles and amphibians. Houghton Mifflin Co., Boston, xv+366 pp.
1960. The queen snake, *Natrix septemvittata*, in the interior highlands of Arkansas and Missouri, with comments upon similar disjunct distribution. Proc. Acad. Nat. Sci. Philadelphia, 112:25-40.
1975. A field guide to reptiles and amphibians of eastern and central North America. Houghton Mifflin Co., Boston, xviii+429 pp.
CONANT, R., *et al.*
1956. Common names for North American amphibians and reptiles. Copeia, 1956:172-185.
CUELLAR, H. S.
1971. Levels of genetic compatibility of *Rana areolata* with southwestern members of the *Rana pipiens* complex (Anura: Ranidae). Evolution, 25:399-409.
DICKERSON, M. C.
1907. The frog book. Doubleday, Page and Co., N.Y., xvii+253 pp.
DOWLING, H. G.
1956. Geographic relations of Ozarkian amphibians and reptiles. Southwest. Nat., 1:174-189.
DUNDEE, H. A.
1965a. *Eurycea multiplicata* (Cope) many-ribbed salamander. Cat. Am. Amphib. Rept., 21.1-21.2.

1965b. *Eurycea tynerensis* Moore and Hughes. Cat. Am. Amphib. Rept., 22.1-22.2.

1971. *Cryptobranchus* and *C. alleganiensis.* Cat. Am. Amphib. Rept., 101.1-101.4.

DUNLAP, D. G. and K. C. KRUSE.

1976. Frogs of the *Rana pipiens* complex in the northern and central plains states. Southwest. Nat., 20:559-571.

DUNN, E. R.

1940. The races of *Ambystoma tigrinum.* Copeia, 1940:154-162.

EASTERLA, D. A.

1968. Melanistic spotted salamanders in northeast Arkansas. Herpetologica, 24:330-331.

ELDER, W. H.

1945. The spadefoot toad in Illinois. Copeia, 1945:122.

FIRSCHEIN, I. L.

1951. The range of *Cryptobranchus bishopi* and remarks on the distribution of the genus *Cryptobranchus.* Am. Midl. Nat., 45:455-459.

FITCH, H. S.

1956. A field study of the Kansas ant-eating frog, *Gastrophryne olivacea.* Univ. Kansas Publ. Mus. Nat. Hist., 8:275-306.

GARTON, J. S. and R. A. BRANDON.

1975. Reproductive ecology of the green treefrog, *Hyla cinerea,* in southern Illinois (Anura: Hylidae). Herpetologica, 31:150-161.

GEHLBACH, F. R.

1967. *Ambystoma tigrinum* (Green) Tiger salamander. Cat. Am. Amphib. Rept., 52.1-52.4.

GEHLBACH, F. R., R. GORDON and J. B. JORDAN.

1973. Aestivation of the salamander, *Siren intermedia.* Am. Midl. Nat. 82:455-463.

GEHLBACH, F. R. and B. WALKER.

1970. Acoustic behavior of the aquatic salamander, *Siren intermedia.* BioScience 20:1107-1108.

GOIN, C. J.

1942. Description of a new race of *Siren intermedia* Le Conte. Ann Carnegie Mus., 29:211-217.

HANSEN, K. I.

1958. Breeding pattern of the eastern spadefoot toad. Herpetologica, 14:57-67.

HARRISON, J. R.

1973. Observations on the life history and ecology of *Eurycea quadridigitata* (Holbrook). HISS News. J., 1:57-58.

HECHT, M. K.

1958. A synopsis of the mud puppies of eastern North America. Proc. Staten Island Inst. Arts Letters, 21:1-38.

HIGHTON, R.

1959. The inheritance of the color phase of *Plethodon cinereus.* Copeia, 1959:33-37.

1962a. Revision of North American salamanders of the genus *Plethodon.* Bull. Florida State Mus., 6:235-367.

1962b. Geograph variation in the life history of the slimy salamander. Copeia, 1962:597-613.

HIGHTON, R. and P. WEBSTER.

1976. Geographic protein variation and divergence in populations of the salamander *Plethodon cinereus.* Evolution, 30:33-45.

HOLBROOK, J. E.

1842. North American herpetology, 2nd ed., 5 Vol. J. Dobson, Philadelphia [reprint ed., 1976, SSAR].

HOLMAN, J. A., H. O. JACKSON and W. H. HILL.
1964. *Pseudacris streckeri illinoensis* Smith from extreme southern Illinois. Herpetologica, 20:205.

HOYT, D. L.
1960. Mating behavior and eggs of the plains spadefoot. Herpetologica, 16:199-201.

HUTCHISON, V. H.
1956. Notes on the plethodontid salamanders, *Eurycea lucifuga* (Rafinesque) and *Eurycea longicauda longicauda* (Green). Occas. Pap. Natl. Speleol. Soc., 3:1-24.
1958. The distribution and ecology of the cave salamander, *Eurycea lucifuga*. Ecol. Monogr., 28:1-20.
1966. *Eurycea lucifuga* (Rafinesque). Cat. Am. Amphib. Rept., 24.1-24.2.

HUTCHISON, V. H. and L. G. HILL.
1976. Thermal selection in the hellbender, *Cryptobranchus alleganiensis*, and the mudpuppy, *Necturus maculosus*. Herpetologica, 32:327-331.

IRELAND, P. H.
1970. Systematics, reproduction, and demography of the salamander *Eurycea multiplicata*. Ph.D. thesis, Univ. Ark., Fayetteville, 127 pp.
1974. Reproductive and larval development of the dark-sided salamander, *Eurycea longicauda melanopleura* (Green). Herpetologica, 30:338-343.
1976. Reproduction and larval development of the gray-bellied salamander *Eurycea multiplicata griseogaster*. Herpetologica, 32:233-238.

JAMESON, E. W., JR.
1947. The food of the western cricket frog. Copeia, 1947:212.

JOHNSON, B. K. and J. L. CHRISTIANSEN.
1976. The food and food habits of Blanchard's cricket frog, *Acris crepitans blanchardi* (Amphibia, Anura, Hylidae), in Iowa. J. Herp., 10:63-74.

JOHNSON, C.
1966. Species recognition in the *Hyla versicolor* complex. Texas J. Sci., 18:361-364.

JOHNSON, T. R., R. N. BADER and D. J. COXWELL.
1975. Amphibians and reptiles in captivity. St. Louis Herp. Soc., Spec. Issue No. 2, iii+38 pp.

LITTLEJOHN, M. J. and R. S. OLDHAM.
1968. *Rana pipiens* complex: Mating call structure and taxonomy. Science, 162:1003-1005.

LYNCH, J. D.
1965. Rediscovery of the four-toed salamander, *Hemidactylium scutatum*, in Illinois: a relict population. Herpetologica, 21:151-153.

MARR, J. C.
1944. Notes on amphibians and reptiles from the central United States. Am. Midl. Nat., 32:478-490.

MARTOF, B. S.
1970. *Rana sylvatica* Le Conte Wood frog. Cat. Am. Amphib. Rept., 86.1-86.4.
1973. *Siren intermedia* Le Conte Lesser sirens. Cat. Am. Amphib. Rept., 127.1-127.3.

MECHAM, J. S.
1954. Geographic variation in the Green frog, *Rana clamitans* Latreille. Texas J. Sci., 6:1-24.

1967. *Notophthalmus viridescens* (Rafinesque) Newt. Cat. Am. Amphib. Rept., 53.1-53.4.

MECHAM, J. S., M. J. LITTLEJOHN, R. S. OLDHAM, L. E. BROWN and J. R. BROWN.
1973. A new species of leopard frog (*Rana pipiens* complex) from the plains of the central United States. Occas. Pap. Mus. Texas Tech Univ., 18:1-11.

MITTLEMAN, M. B.
1967. *Manculus* and *M. quadridigitatus.* Cat. Am. Amphib. Rept., 44.1-44.2.

MORRIS, P. A.
1944. They hop and crawl. The Jaques Cattel Press. York, Pa., xiv+253 pp.

MOUNT, R. H.
1975. The reptiles and amphibians of Alabama. Auburn Univ., Auburn, Ala., viii+347 pp.

NEILL, W. T.
1963. *Hemidactylium scutatum* (Schlegel) Four-toed salamander. Cat. Am. Amphib. Rept., 2.1-2.2.

NELSON, C. E.
1972a. *Gastrophryne carolinensis* (Holbrook) Eastern narrow-mouthed toad. Cat. Am. Amphib. Rept., 120.1-120.4.
1972b. Systematic studies of the North American microhylid genus *Gastrophryne.* J. Herp., 6:111-137.
1972c. *Gastrophryne olivacea* (Hallowell) Western narrow-mouthed toad. Cat. Am. Amphib. Rept., 122.1-122.4.

NICKERSON, M. A. and C. E. MAYS.
1973. The hellbenders. Milwaukee Pub. Mus. Publ. Biol. Geol. 1, viii+106 pp.

NOBLE, G. K.
1931. The biology of the Amphibia. McGraw-Hill, New York, xiii+577 pp.

OLIVER, J. A.
1955. The natural history of North American amphibians and reptiles. D. Van Nostrand Co., Inc., Princeton, New Jersey. ix+359 pp.

ORTON, G.
1942. Notes on the larvae of certain species of *Ambystoma.* Copeia, 1942:170-172.

PACE, A. E.
1974. Systematic and biological studies of the leopard frogs (*Rana pipiens* complex) of the United States. Mus. Zool. Univ. Michigan Misc. Publ., 148:1-140.

PARMALEE, P. W.
1954. Amphibians of Illinois. Story of Illinois No. 10, Illinois State Mus., 38 pp.

PETERS, J. A.
1946. Records of certain North American salamanders. Copeia, 1946:106.

RALIN, D. B.
1968. Ecological and reproductive differentiation in the cryptic species of the *Hyla versicolor* complex (Hylidae). Southwest. Nat., 13:283-299.

RAVELING, D. G.
1965. Variation in a sample of *Bufo americanus* from southwestern Illinois. Herpetologica, 21:219-225.

REGAN, G. T.
1972. Natural and man-made conditions determining the range of *Acris*

crepitans in the Missouri River basin. Ph.D. Thesis, Univ. Kan., 130 pp.

RHODES, R.
1974. The Ozarks. Time-Life Books, Time Inc., N.Y., 184 pp.

RICHMOND, N. D.
1947. Life history of *Scaphiopus holbrookii holbrookii* (Harlan). Part I. Larval development and behavior. Ecology, 28:53-67.

SALTHE, S. N.
1973. *Amphiuma tridactylum* Cuvier Three-toed Congo eel. Cat. Am. Amphib. Rept., 149.1-149.3.

SANDERS, H. O.
1970. Pesticide toxicities to tadpoles of the western chorus from *Pseudacris triseriata* and Fowler's toad *Bufo woodhousii fowleri*. Copeia, 1970:246-251.

SCHAAF, R. T. and P. W. SMITH.
1970. Geographic variation in the pickerel frog. Herpetologica, 26:240-254.
1971. *Rana palustris* Le Conte Pickerel frog. Cat. Am. Amphib. Rept., 117.1-117.3.

SCHMIDT, K. P.
1953. A checklist of North American amphibians and reptiles. Sixth ed., ASIH, Chicago, viii+280 pp.

SCOTT, F. and R. M. JOHNSON
1972. Geographic distribution: *Ambystoma texanum*. Herp. Rev., 4:95.

SHOOP, C. R.
1964. *Ambystoma talpoideum* (Holbrook) Mole salamander. Cat. Am. Amphib. Rept., 8.1-8.2.

SMITH, H. M.
1937. Notes on *Scaphiopus hurterii*. Herpetologica, 1:104-108.
1950. Handbook of amphibians and reptiles of Kansas. Misc. Publ. Univ. Kansas Mus. Nat. Hist., 2:1-336.

SMITH, P. W.
1961. The amphibians and reptiles of Illinois. Bull. Illinois Nat. Hist. Surv., 28:1-298.
1963. *Plethodon cinereus* (Green) Red-backed and lead-backed salamander. Cat. Am. Amphib. Rept., 5.1-5.3.
1966a. *Hyla avivoca* Viosca Bird-voiced treefrog. Cat. Am. Amphib. Rept., 28.1-28.2.
1966b. *Pseudacris streckeri* Wright and Wright Strecker's chorus frog. Cat. Am. Amphib. Rept., 27.1-27.2.

SMITH, P. W. and D. M. SMITH.
1952. The relationships of the chorus frogs, *Pseudacris nigrita feriarum* and *Pseudacris n. triseriata*. Am. Midl. Nat., 48:165-180.

SNYDER, D. H.
1972. Amphibians and reptiles of Land Between the Lakes. Tenn. Valley Auth., 90 pp.

SPOTILA, J. R. and R. J. BEUMER.
1970. The breeding habits of the ringed salamander, *Ambystoma annulatum* (Cope), in northwestern Arkansas. Am. Midl. Nat., 84:77-89.

TANNER, W. W.
1950. Notes on the habits of *Microhyla carolinensis olivacea* (Hallowell). Herpetologica, 6:47-48.

THUROW, G. R.
1956. Comparison of two species of salamanders, *P. cinereus* and *P. dorsalis*. Herpetologica, 12:177-182.
1957. Relationships of the red-backed and zigzag plethodons in the west.

Herpetologica, 13:91-99.

1966. *Plethodon dorsalis* Cope Zigzag salamander. Cat. Am. Amphib. Rept., 29.1-29.3.

1968. On the small black *Plethodon* problem. W. Illinois Univ. Ser. Biol. Sci. 6:1-48.

TRAPP, M. M.

1956. Range and natural history of the ringed salamander, *Ambystoma annulatum* Cope (Ambystomatidae). Southwest. Nat., 1:78-82.

TURNIPSEED, G.

1976. Geographic distribution: *Hyla avivoca avivoca* (Western Bird-voiced Treefrog). Herp. Review, 7:178-179.

VALENTINE, B. D.

1964. A preliminary key to the families of salamanders and sirenids with gills or gill slits. Copeia, 1964:582-583.

VIPARINA, S. and J. J. JUST.

1975. The life period, growth and differentiation of *Rana catesbeiana* larvae occurring in nature. Copeia, 1975:103-109.

VOLPE, E. P.

1955. Intensity of reproductive isolation between sympatric and allopatric populations of *Bufo americanus* and *Bufo fowleri*. Am. Nat., 89: 303-317.

WASSERMAN, A. O.

1968. *Scaphiopus holbrookii* (Harlan) Eastern spadefoot toad. Cat. Am. Amphib. Rept., 70.1-70.4.

WRIGHT, A. H. and A. A. WRIGHT.

1949. Handbook of frogs and toads of the United States and Canada. Comstock Pub. Assoc., Cornell Univ. Press. Ithaca, N.Y., vi+286 pp.

WRIGHT, A. M.

1929. Synopsis and descriptions of North American tadpoles. Proc. U.S. Nat. Mus., 74 (11):1-70.

BIBLIOGRAPHY
PART II. MISSOURI REFERENCES

This list consists of publications which specifically treat the amphibians (and/or reptiles) which have been studied in Missouri, and are provided for those who wish to learn more about the herpetofauna of Missouri.

ALT, A.

1910. On the histology of the eye of *Typhlotriton spelaeus*, from Marble Cave, Mo. Trans. St. Louis Acad. Sci., 19:83-96.

ANDERSON, P.

1942. Amphibians and reptiles of Jackson Co., Missouri. Bull. Chicago Acad. Sci. 6:203-220.

1945. New herpetological records for Missouri. Bull. Chicago Acad. Sci. 7:271-275.

1950. A range extension for the ringed salamander, *Ambystoma annulatum* Cope. Herpetologica, 6:55.

1965. The reptiles of Missouri. Univ. Mo. Press, Columbia, Mo., xxiii+ 330 pp.

BESHARSE, J. C. and R. A. BRANDON.

1974a. Postembryonic eye degeneration in the troglobitic salamander *Typhlotriton spelaeus*. J. Morph. 144:381-405.

1974b. Size and growth of the eyes of the troglobitic salamander *Typhlotriton spelaeus.* Int. J. Speleol., 6:255-264.

BLANCHARD, F. N.
1925. A collection of amphibians and reptiles from southeastern Missouri and southern Illinois. Michigan Acad. Sci. Arts Letters Pap., 4:533-541.

BOYER, D. A. and A. A. HEINZE.
1934. An annotated list of the amphibians and reptiles of Jefferson County, Missouri. Trans. St. Louis Acad. Sci., 28:185-201.

BRANDON, R. A.
1966. A reevaluation of the status of the salamander, *Typhlotriton nereus* Bishop. Copeia, 1966:555-561.
1971. Correlation of seasonal abundance with feeding and reproductive activity in the grotto salamander (*Typhlotriton spelaeus*). Am. Midl. Nat., 86:93-100.

CONWAY, C. H. and D. E. METTER.
1967. Glands associated with breeding in *Microhyla carolinensis.* Copeia, 1967:672-673.

DUNDEE, H. A. and D. S. DUNDEE.
1965. Observations on the systematics and ecology of *Cryptobranchus* from the Ozark Plateaus of Missouri and Arkansas. Copeia, 1965: 369-370.

DYRKACZ, S. E.
1973. Geographic distribution: *Gastrophryne carolinensis* (eastern narrow-mouthed toad). HISS News-J., 1:152.

EASTERLA, D. A.
1970. Albinistic small-mouthed salamander from southeastern Missouri. Trans. Missouri Acad. Sci., 4:93-94.
1971. A breeding concentration of four-toed salamanders, *Hemidactylium scutatum,* in southeastern Missouri. J. Herp., 5:194-195.
1972. Herpetological records for northwest Missouri. Trans. Missouri Acad. Sci., 6:158-160.

EASTERLA, D. A. and H. GREGORY.
1967. First record of the mole salamander for Missouri. Herpetologica, 23:239-240.

FUNK, R. S.
1974. Addendum to a checklist of Missouri amphibians and reptiles. St. Louis Herp. Soc. Newsl., 1:2-5.
1975. The leopard frogs of Missouri. St. Louis Herp. Soc. Newsl., 2:2-6.

HENNING, W. L.
1938. Amphibians and reptiles of a 2,220-acre tract in central Missouri. Copeia, 1938:91-92.

HURTER, J.
1893. Catalogue of reptiles and batrachians found in the vicinity of St. Louis, Mo. Trans. St. Louis Acad. Sci., 6:251-261.
1897. A contribution to the herpetology of Missouri. Trans. St. Louis Acad. Sci., 7:499-503.
1903. A second contribution to the herpetology of Missouri. Trans. St. Louis Acad. Sci., 13:77-86.
1911. Herpetology of Missouri. Trans. St. Louis Acad. Sci., 20:59-274.

JOHNSON, T. R.
1974a. A checklist of Missouri toads and frogs. St. Louis Herp. Soc. Newsl., 1:6-7.
1974b. A preliminary checklist of the salamanders of Missouri. St. Louis Herp. Soc. Newsl., 1:8-9.

1975a. Record size mudpuppy for Missouri. St. Louis Herp. Soc. Newsl., 2:3-4.

1975b. Fall choruses of *Hyla crucifer* in Missouri. St. Louis Herp. Soc. Newsl., 2:5-6.

JOHNSON, T. R. and R. N. BADER.
1974. Annotated checklist of Missouri amphibians and reptiles. St. Louis Herp. Soc. Spec. Issue 1:1-16.

METTER, D. E., W. R. MORRIS and D. A. KANGAS.
1970. Great plains anurans in central Missouri. Copeia, 1970:780-781.

MITTLEMAN, M. B.
1950. Cavern-dwelling salamanders of the Ozark Plateau. Bull. Nat. Speleol. Soc., 12:1-14.

MYERS, C. W.
1958. Amphibians in Missouri Caves. Herpetologica, 14:35-36.

1959. Amphibians and reptiles of Montauk State Park and vicinity, Dent County, Missouri. Trans. Kansas Acad. Sci., 62:88-90.

NICKERSON, M. A. and R. KRAGER.
1971. Noteworthy records of Missouri reptiles. Trans. Kansas Acad. Sci., 74:99-101.

1972. Additional noteworthy records of Missouri amphibians and reptiles with a possible addition to the herpetofauna. Trans. Kansas Acad. Sci., 75:276-277.

NICKERSON, M. A. and C. E. MAYS.
1973. A study of the Ozark hellbender *Cryptobranchus alleganiensis bishopi.* Ecology, 54:1164-1165.

ORTON, G. L.
1951. Notes on some tadpoles from southwestern Missouri. Copeia, 1951: 71-72.

PINGLETON, M., J. ROTH and A. ROGERS.
1975. Bullfrog found in Cliff Cave. St. Louis Herp. Soc. Newsl., 2:14.

SCHROEDER, E. E.
1975. The reproductive cycle in the male bullfrog, *Rana catesbeiana* in Missouri. Trans. Kansas Acad. Sci., 77:31-35.

SCHROEDER, E. E. and T. S. BASKETT.
1965. Frogs and toads of Missouri. The Conservationist, Mo. Conservation Comm., 26:15-18.

SMITH, P. W.
1948. Food habits of cave dwelling amphibians. Herpetologica, 4:205-208.

1956. A second record of *Hemidactylium scutatum* in Missouri. Trans. Kansas Acad. Sci., 59:463-464.

STEJNEGER, L.
1893. Preliminary description of a new genus and species of blind cave salamander from North America. Proc. U.S. Nat. Mus. (for 1892), 15:115-117.

WATKINS, L. C.
1969. A third record of the four-toed salamander, *Hemidactylium scutatum,* in Missouri. Trans. Kansas Acad. Sci., 72:264-265.

WILEY, J. R.
1968. Guide to the amphibians of Missouri. Missouri Speleology, 1:132-172.

WILLS, Y. L., D. L. MOYLE and T. S. BASKETT.
1956. Emergence, breeding, hibernation, movement and transformation of the bullfrog, *Rana catesbeiana* in Missouri. Copeia, 1956:30-41.

INDEX TO SCIENTIFIC AND COMMON NAMES

Acris crepitans blanchardi _____ 9, 15, 80

alleganiensis bishopi, Cryptobranchus _____ 4, 8, 18, 19, 20

alleganiensis, Cryptobranchus alleganiensis _____ 8, 11, 18, 19, 20

Ambystoma _____ 8, 12, 24, 25, 27, 29, 31, 33, 35

    annulatum _____ 8, 12, 25

    maculatum _____ 8, 12, 24, 27

    opacum _____ 8, 12, 29

    talpoideum _____ 5, 8, 12, 31

    texanum _____ 8, 12, 33

    tigrinum tigrinum _____ 8, 12, 35

Ambystomatidae _____ 8, 24

americanus, Bufo americanus _____ 9, 14, 70, 72

americanus charlesmithi, Bufo _____ 9, 14, 71, 72, 73

American Toad _____ 9, 14, 70, 72, 73, 78

    Dwarf _____ 9, 14, 71, 72, 73

Amphiumidae _____ 8, 41

Amphiuma _____ 41, 42, 43

    One-toed _____ 41

    Two-toed _____ 41

    Three-toed _____ 5, 8, 11, 41, 42, 43

Amphiuma _____ 5, 8, 11, 41, 42, 43

    means _____ 41

    pholeter _____ 41

    tridactylium _____ 5, 8, 11, 41, 42, 43

Andrias _____ 18

    davidianus _____ 18

    japonicus _____ 18

angusticlavius, Plethodon dorsalis _____ 8, 13, 54

areolata circulosa, Rana _____ 4, 9, 16, 100

avivoca, Hyla avivoca _____ 116

Bird-voiced Treefrog, Western _____ 116

bishopi, Cryptobranchus alleganiensis _____ 4, 8, 18, 19, 20

bislineata cirrigera, Eurycea _____ 116

bislineata, Eurycea bislineata _____ 116

blairi, Rana _____ 4, 9, 17, 102, 108, 111

blanchardi, Acris crepitans _____ 9, 15, 80

Blanchard's Cricket Frog _____ 9, 15, 80, 81

bombifrons, Scaphiopus _____ 4, 9, 14, 66

Bufo _____ 9, 14, 15, 70, 71, 72, 73, 74, 76, 77, 78

    americanus _____ 9, 14, 70, 71, 72, 73

    americanus americanus _____ 9, 14, 70, 72

    americanus charlesmithi _____ 9, 14, 71, 72, 73

    cognatus _____ 9, 15, 74

    woodhousei fowleri _____ 9, 15, 73, 77

    woodhousei woodhousei _____ 4, 9, 15, 76, 77

Bufonidae _____ 9, 65, 70

Bullfrog _____ 9, 16, 99, 104, 105

carolinensis, Gastrophryne _____ 9, 16, 94, 95, 98

catesbeiana, Rana _____ 9, 16, 99, 104
Cave Salamander _____ 8, 13, 47, 48
Central Newt _____ 8, 11, 37, 38, 39, 40
charlesmithi, Bufo americanus _____ 9, 14, 71, 72, 73
Chinese Giant Salamander _____ 18
Chorus Frog
    Illinois _____ 9, 15, 90, 91
    Upland _____ 9, 15, 93
    Western _____ 9, 15, 92, 93
chrysoscelis, Hyla _____ 9, 16, 87, 89
cinerea, Hyla _____ 3, 5, 9, 15, 82
cinereus, Plethodon cinereus _____ 59
cirrigera, Eurycea bislineata _____ 116
clamitans clamitans, Rana _____ 9, 16, 107
clamitans melanota, Rana _____ 9, 16, 106, 107
clamitans, Rana _____ 9, 16, 106, 107
cognatus, Bufo _____ 9, 15, 74
conanti, Desmognathus fuscus _____ 116
Cope's Gray Treefrog _____ 9, 16, 88, 89
Crawfish Frog, Northern _____ 4, 9, 16, 100, 101
crepitans blanchardi, Acris _____ 9, 15, 80
Cricket Frog, Blanchard's _____ 9, 15, 80, 81
crucifer, Hyla crucifer _____ 3, 9, 15, 80
Cryptobranchidae _____ 8, 18
Cryptobranchus alleganiensis _____ 8, 11, 18, 19, 20
    alleganiensis _____ 8, 11, 18, 19, 20
    bishopi _____ 4, 8, 18, 19, 20
Dark-sided Salamander _____ 8, 13, 46
davidianus, Andrias _____ 18
Desmognathus fuscus conanti _____ 116
dorsalis angusticlavius, Plethodon _____ 8, 13, 54
Dusky Salamander, Spotted _____ 116
Dwarf American Toad _____ 9, 14, 71, 72, 73
Dwarf Salamander _____ 116
Dwarf Siren _____ 21
Eastern
    Gray Treefrog _____ 9, 16, 79, 87, 88, 89
    Narrow-mouthed Toad _____ 9, 16, 94, 95, 96
    Spadefoot Toad _____ 9, 14, 65, 68, 69
    Tiger Salamander _____ 8, 12, 35, 36
Eurycea _____ 8, 12, 45, 46, 47, 49, 51, 116
    bislineata bislineata _____ 116
    bislineata cirrigera _____ 116
    longicauda longicauda _____ 8, 13, 45, 46
    longicauda melanopleura _____ 8, 13, 46
    lucifuga _____ 8, 13, 47
    multiplicata griseogaster _____ 4, 8, 12, 44, 49
    quadridigitatus _____ 116
    tynerensis _____ 8, 12, 51

Four-toed Salamander _____ 8, 11, 52, 53
fowleri, Bufo woodhousei _____ 9, 15, 73, 77
Fowler's Toad _____ 9, 15, 77, 78
Frog
    Blanchard's Cricket _____ 9, 15, 80, 81
    Bronze _____ 9, 16, 107
    Bullfrog _____ 9, 16, 99, 104, 105
    Green _____ 9, 16, 106, 107
    Illinois Chorus _____ 9, 15, 90, 91
    Northern Crawfish _____ 4, 9, 16, 100, 101
    Northern Leopard _____ 116
    Pickerel _____ 9, 17, 108, 109
    Plains Leopard _____ 4, 9, 17, 102, 103, 108
    Southern Leopard _____ 9, 17, 102, 103, 108, 111, 112, 113
    Upland Chorus _____ 3, 9, 15, 93
    Western Chorus _____ 3, 9, 15, 92, 93
    Wood _____ 9, 16, 99, 114, 115
fuscus conanti, Desmognathus _____ 116
Gastrophryne _____ 9, 16, 94, 95, 96, 97, 98
    carolinensis _____ 9, 16, 94, 95, 98
    olivacea _____ 4, 9, 16, 95, 96, 97, 98
Giant Salamander _____ 18
    Chinese _____ 18
    Japanese _____ 18
glutinosus, Plethodon glutinosus _____ 8, 13, 56
Gray-bellied Salamander _____ 4, 8, 12, 44, 49, 50
Gray Treefrog
    Cope's _____ 9, 16, 88, 89
    Eastern _____ 9, 16, 79, 87, 88, 89
Great Plains
    Narrow-mouthed Toad _____ 4, 9, 16, 96, 97, 98
    Toad _____ 9, 15, 74, 75
Green Frog _____ 9, 16, 106, 107
Green Treefrog _____ 5, 9, 15, 82, 83, 84
Greater Siren _____ 21
griseogaster, Eurycea multiplicata _____ 4, 8, 12, 44, 49
Grotto Salamander _____ 4, 8, 13, 60, 61
Hellbender _____ 8, 11, 18, 19, 20
Hellbender, Ozark _____ 4, 8, 18, 19, 20
Hemidactylium scutatum _____ 8, 11, 52, 53
holbrookii, Scaphiopus holbrookii _____ 9, 14, 65, 68
hurterii, Scaphiopus holbrookii _____ 116
Hurter's Spadefoot Toad _____ 116
Hyla _____ 3, 9, 15, 16, 79, 82, 84, 85, 86, 87, 89
    avivoca avivoca _____ 116
    cinerea _____ 3, 5, 9, 15, 82
    crucifer crucifer _____ 3, 9, 15, 85
    chrysoscelis _____ 9, 16, 87, 89
    versicolor versicolor _____ 3, 9, 16, 79, 87, 89
Hylidae _____ 3, 9, 79
illinoensis, Pseudacris streckeri _____ 9, 15, 90

Illinois Chorus Frog _____ 9, 15, 90, 91
intermedia nettingi, Siren _____ 8, 11, 21, 22, 23
Japanese Giant Salamander _____ 18
japonicus, Andrias _____ 18
lacertina, Siren _____ 21
Leopard Frog _____ 9, 17, 102, 103, 108, 111, 112, 113
    Plains _____ 4, 9, 17, 102, 103, 108
    Northern _____ 116
    Southern _____ 9, 17, 102, 103, 108, 111, 112, 113
longicauda, Eurycea longicauda _____ 8, 13, 45, 46
longicauda melanopleura, Eurycea _____ 8, 13, 46
Long-tailed Salamander _____ 8, 13, 45, 46
louisianensis
    Necturus maculosus _____ 8, 64
    Notophthalmus viridescens _____ 8, 11, 37, 38
lucifuga, Eurycea _____ 8, 13, 47
maculatum, Ambystoma _____ 8, 12, 24, 27
maculosus
    louisianensis, Necturus _____ 8, 64
    maculosus, Necturus _____ 8, 64
Marbled Salamander _____ 8, 12, 29, 30
means, Amphiuma _____ 41
Megophryinae _____ 65
melanopleura, Eurycea longicauda _____ 8, 13, 46
melanota, Rana clamitans _____ 9, 16, 106, 107
Mole Salamander _____ 5, 8, 12, 31, 32
Mudpuppy _____ 8, 11, 62, 63, 64
multiplicata griseogaster, Eurycea _____ 4, 8, 12, 44, 49
Narrow-mouthed Toad
    Eastern _____ 9, 16, 94, 95, 96
    Great Plains _____ 9, 16, 96, 97, 98
Necturus _____ 8, 11, 62, 63, 64
    maculosus _____ 8, 11, 63, 64
    maculosus louisianensis _____ 8, 64
    maculosus maculosus _____ 8, 64
Northern
    Crawfish Frog _____ 4, 9, 16, 100, 101
    Leopard Frog _____ 116
    Spring Peeper _____ 9, 15, 85, 86
    Two-lined Salamander _____ 116
Notophthalmus viridescens louisianenis _____ 8, 11, 37, 38
Olm _____ 62
Oklahoma Salamander _____ 8, 12, 51
olivacea, Gastrophryne _____ 4, 9, 16, 95, 96, 97, 98
One-toed Amphiuma _____ 41
opacum, Ambystoma _____ 8, 12, 29
Ozark
    Hellbender _____ 4, 8, 18, 19, 20
    Red-backed Salamander _____ 8, 13, 54, 55

palustris, Rana _____ 9, 17, 108, 111
Peeper, Northern Spring _____ 8, 15, 85, 86
Pelobatidae _____ 8, 65
Pelobatinae _____ 8, 65
pholeter, Amphiuma _____ 41
Pickerel Frog _____ 9, 17, 108, 109, 110, 111
pipiens, Rana _____ 116
Plains
    Leopard Frog _____ 4, 9, 17, 102, 103, 108
    Spadefoot Toad _____ 4, 9, 14, 66, 67
Plethodon _____ 8, 13, 54, 55, 56, 58, 59
    cinereus cinereus _____ 59
    dorsalis angusticlavius _____ 8, 13, 54
    dorsalis dorsalis _____ 55
    glutinosus glutinosus _____ 8, 13, 56
    serratus _____ 8, 13, 54, 58, 59
Plethodontidae _____ 8, 44
Proteidae _____ 8, 62
Proteus _____ 62
Pseudacris _____ 3, 9, 15, 79, 90, 92, 93
    streckeri illinoensis _____ 9, 15, 90
    triseriata feriarum _____ 3, 9, 15, 93
    triseriata triseriata _____ 3, 9, 15, 92, 93
Pseudobranchus _____ 21
quadridigitatus, Eurycea _____ 116
Rana _____ 9, 16, 17, 99, 100, 101, 102, 103, 104, 106, 107, 108, 111, 114, 116
    areolata circulosa _____ 4, 9, 16, 100
    blairi _____ 4, 9, 17, 102, 108, 111
    catesbeiana _____ 9, 16, 99, 104
    clamitans clamitans _____ 9, 16, 107
    clamitans melanota _____ 9, 16, 106, 107
    palustris _____ 9, 17, 108, 111
    pipiens _____ 116
    sphenocephala _____ 9, 17, 102, 103, 108, 111, 112
    sylvatica _____ 9, 16, 99, 114
    utricularia _____ 112
Ranidae _____ 3, 9, 99
Ringed Salamander _____ 8, 12, 25, 26
Salamander
    Cave _____ 8, 12, 51, 52
    Chinese Giant _____ 18
    Dark-sided _____ 8, 13, 46
    Dwarf _____ 116
    Eastern Tiger _____ 8, 12, 35, 36
    Four-toed _____ 8, 12, 52, 53
    Gray-bellied _____ 4, 8, 12, 44, 49, 50
    Grotto _____ 4, 8, 13, 60, 61
    Japanese Giant _____ 18
    Long-tailed _____ 8, 13, 45, 46
    Marbled _____ 8, 12, 29, 30
    Mole _____ 5, 8, 12, 31, 32
    Oklahoma _____ 8, 12, 51

Ozark Red-backed _____ 8, 13, 54, 55
Northern Two-lined _____ 116
Ringed _____ 8, 12, 25, 26
Slimy _____ 8, 13, 56, 57
Small-mouthed _____ 8, 12, 33, 34
Southern Red-backed _____ 8, 13, 54, 58, 59
Southern Two-lined _____ 116
Spotted Dusky _____ 116
Spotted _____ 8, 12, 24, 27, 28
Salamandridae _____ 8, 37
Scaphiopus _____ 9, 14, 65, 66, 68
    bombifrons _____ 4, 9, 14, 66
    holbrookii holbrookii _____ 9, 14, 65, 68
    holbrookii hurterii _____ 116
scutatum, Hemidactylium _____ 8, 11, 52, 53
serratus, Plethodon _____ 8, 13, 54, 58, 59
Sirenidae _____ 8, 21
Siren intermedia nettingi _____ 8, 11, 21, 22, 23
    lacertina _____ 21
Siren _____ 8, 11, 21, 22, 23
    Dwarf _____ 21
    Greater _____ 21
    Western Lesser _____ 8, 11, 21, 22, 23
Slimy Salamander _____ 8, 13, 56, 57
Small-mouthed Salamander _____ 8, 12, 33, 34
Southern
    Leopard Frog _____ 9, 17, 102, 103, 108, 111, 112, 113
    Red-backed Salamander _____ 8, 13, 54, 58, 59
    Two-lined Salamander _____ 116
Spadefoot Toad
    Eastern _____ 9, 14, 65, 68, 69
    Hurter's _____ 116
    Plains _____ 4, 9, 14, 66, 67
spelaeus, Typhlotriton _____ 4, 8, 13, 60
sphenocephala, Rana _____ 9, 17, 102, 103, 108, 111, 112
Spotted
    Dusky Salamander _____ 116
    Salamander _____ 8, 12, 24, 27, 28
Spring Peeper, Northern _____ 9, 15, 85, 86
streckeri illinoensis, Pseudacris _____ 9, 15, 90
sylvatica, Rana _____ 9, 16, 99, 114
talpoideum, Ambystoma _____ 5, 8, 12, 31
Taricha _____ 37
texanum, Ambystoma _____ 8, 12, 33
Three-toed Amphiuma _____ 5, 8, 11, 41, 42, 43
Tiger Salamander, Eastern _____ 8, 12, 35, 36
tigrinum, Ambystoma tigrinum _____ 8, 12, 35
Toad
    American _____ 9, 14, 70, 72, 73, 78
    Dwarf American _____ 9, 14, 71, 72, 73
    Eastern Narrow-mouthed _____ 9, 16, 94, 95, 96

Eastern Spadefoot _____ 9, 14, 65, 68, 69
Fowler's _____ 9, 15, 77, 78
Great Plains Narrow-mouthed _____ 9, 16, 96, 97, 98
Great Plains _____ 9, 15, 74, 75
Hurter's Spadefoot _____ 116
Plains Spadefoot _____ 4, 9, 14, 66, 67
Woodhouse's _____ 4, 9, 15, 76, 77, 78
Treefrog
Cope's Gray _____ 9, 16, 88, 89
Eastern Gray _____ 9, 16, 79, 87, 88, 89
Green _____ 5, 9, 15, 82, 83, 84
Western Bird-voiced _____ 116
tridactylium, Amphiuma _____ 8, 11, 41, 42, 43
triseriata feriarum, Pseudacris _____ 3, 9, 15, 93
triseriata, Pseudacris _____ 3, 9, 15, 92, 93
triseriata, Pseudacris triseriata _____ 3, 9, 15, 92, 93
Two-lined Salamander
Northern _____ 116
Southern _____ 116
Two-toed Amphiuma _____ 41
tynerensis, Eurycea _____ 8, 12, 51
Typhlotriton spelaeus _____ 4, 8, 13, 60
utricularia, Rana _____ 112
Upland Chorus Frog _____ 3, 9, 15, 93
versicolor versicolor, Hyla _____ 3, 9, 16, 79, 87, 89
viridescens louisianensis, Notophthalmus _____ 8, 11, 37, 38
Waterdog, Red River _____ 64
Western Bird-voiced Treefrog _____ 116
Western Chorus Frog _____ 3, 9, 15, 92, 93
Western Lesser Siren _____ 8, 11, 21, 22, 23
Wood Frog _____ 9, 16, 99, 114, 115
woodhousei, Bufo _____ 9, 15, 73, 76, 77
woodhousei fowleri, Bufo _____ 9, 15, 73, 77
woodhousei woodhousei, Bufo _____ 4, 9, 15, 76, 77
Woodhouse's Toad _____ 4, 9, 15, 76, 77, 78